♡ DEAREST ALEX..... HAPPY 21ST!!

With all the love in the world from

Mum and Dad xx.

First published in 2014 by Soul Jazz Books, a division of Soul Jazz Records Ltd.

Soul Jazz Records

7 Broadwick Street

London W1F 0DA

England

www.souljazzrecords.co.uk

Design and layout by Adrian Self & Dee Dee Solstice

Edited and introduction by Stuart Baker

Biographies by Chris Menist

Distributed by Thames & Hudson and D.A.P.

ISBN: 978-09572600-1-6

Soul Jazz wish to thank: A special thanks to Stephen Kirkby @ Getty Images, Chris Menist, Karen Tate, Jon Dennis, Angela Scott, Bridget and Rudy, Pete Reilly, Mark Garland at Thames and Hudson, Todd Bradway at DAP, Newton, Rufus and Clover, Julie Vermeille, Conny Dickgreber, Neal Birnie, Nicole McKenzie, Jim Cronshaw, Karl Shale, Wayne Gilbert, Abi Clarke, Scott Bethell, Dean Atkins, Shelley Latimer, Steve Platt, Jeyda Bicer, Theo Leanse, Jonathon Burnip, Pierce Smith, Ingmar Van Wijnsberg, Boudewijn van Wijk, Anders Sjoelin, Lutz Falldorf, Jeffrey Stothers, Maurizio Morozzo, Danilo Durante, Luciano Cantone, Jeremiah Lewis, Matt Fisher, Ernie B, Maria Calero, Jose Santos Luisa Da Silva, Magnus Hogmur, Yves le Carpentier and Ylan Pham.

Chris Menist would like to thank: David Hill and Sarah Menist

Cover images: Elliot Landy/Premium Archive/Getty Images
p. 38, 39: Terence Donovan/Terence Donovan Archive/Getty Images; p. 68, 69: Jan Persson/Premium Archive/Getty images; p. 26, 40, 78, 79: Elliot Landy/Premium Archive/Getty Images; p. 175: Bob Willoughy/ Premium Archive/Getty images; p. 100: Fred W McDarrah/ Premium Archive/Getty images; p. 140, 176: The Estate of David Gahr/ Premium Archive/Getty images.
All other Images via Getty Images

BLACK FIRE! NEW SPIRITS!

IMAGES OF A REVOLUTION RADICAL JAZZ IN THE USA 1960-75

SOUL JAZZ BOOKS

BLACK FIRE! NEW SPIRITS!

IMAGES OF A REVOLUTION RADICAL JAZZ IN THE USA 1960-75

Rosa Louise McCauley Parks (1913-2005), American civil rights activist. Police booking photo taken at the time of her arrest for refusing to give up her seat on a Montgomery, Alabama, bus to a white passenger on 1st December 1955.

From the mid-1950s onwards, the United States government sponsored a number of high profile jazz musicians, including Louis Armstrong (pictured here), Duke Ellington and Dizzy Gillespie to travel the world promoting the cultural, educational and social benefits of living in America, most notably the principle of 'freedom', to audiences abroad.

Jazz … the new thing, the new wave, free jazz, afro-centricity, afro-futurism, space jazz, soul jazz, new black music, post-bop, hard bop, avant-garde, abstract, spiritual, anti-jazz, radical, revolutionary ... While definitions were sometimes hard to pin down, one thing became clear about jazz music in the United States in the 1960s. As Ornette Coleman succinctly framed it in the title of his 1960 album for Atlantic Records: 'This is our music.'

In this most profound of decades, jazz evolved like the head of Medusa, a mass of interweaving narratives, an art form as complex and charged as the environment and era in which it was created. As we look now at this intense period some 50 years hence, what is evident (as was only to precious few at the time) is that these multiple diverse strands and styles, though widely disparate, were nonetheless all simply leaves, branches and boughs of the vast tree of African-American musical expression - jazz.

Certain musicians chose words to signify a new approach, a new way of seeing, in the process liberating both themselves and their music. To the Art Ensemble of Chicago, their music became simply 'great black music'; for Archie Shepp, jazz music was 'black classical music'; in the mind of Albert Ayler it became 'the healing force of the universe'; while John Coltrane's search was for a 'universal sound'.

If we chose to dissect the plethora of stylistic variants that proliferated in jazz music in 1960s, we see how condescending the term 'entertainer' was to many jazz musicians. Instead among them we would find philosophers and theoreticians such as Ornette Coleman, Cecil Taylor or Anthony Braxton – dismantlers and questioners of tradition, creators of new musical forms, influenced by the worlds of European classical, art music, avant-garde and even mathematics. We would find spiritual leaders, most notably the powerhouse that was John Coltrane, and his saints and disciples: Pharoah Sanders, McCoy Tyner, Elvin Jones, Rashied Ali and Alice Coltrane. Mystics and visionaries, primarily the Afro-futurist Sun Ra. Also activists – radicals and polemicists of Afro-centricity such as Archie Shepp, the politicised jazz-poetry and street rap of The Last Poets and Gil Scott-Heron; and community leaders and teachers and collectives such as the Association of Creative Musicians in Chicago, the Black Artists Group in St Louis, the Underground Musicians Association in Los Angeles, the Tribe collective in Detroit and the Jazz Musicians Guild in New York. Also there were the soul jazz and organ combos – Jimmy Smith, Lonnie Smith, Cannonball Adderley – who earthily connected jazz to rhythm and blues, soul and gospel, so popular with the uptown African-American who was sometimes alienated by the avant-gardism that flourished (pretty much solely) in downtown New York City.

Throughout this era critics, audiences, governments, nationalist activists, politicians, academics, diplomats and revolutionaries argued and vied relentlessly and intensely over the ground rules by which jazz should be measured, what its value was, and the criteria by which it should be judged either good or bad. This was often in semantic terms: should jazz be seen as a distinctly American art form, or as an African-American one? What was it that made it 'authentic' or 'inauthentic'? Was free jazz anti-music? Was it Afro-centric ... or too Euro-centric in its aesthetic? Should jazz function as art or entertainment? Should it be revolutionary or sedentary?

In contrast to those involved in these polemical debates, African-American jazz musicians remained confident in the knowledge that the only critic of any note worth listening to was one's own integrity. An artist as otherworldly and liberated as Sun Ra, or as spiritually possessed as John Coltrane, for instance, was never going to be beholden to anything so earthly and mundane as market forces, critical acclaim, peer pressure, stylistic fashions or music industry wisdom.

No, any questions of self-identity for these artists had been worked out many, many years ago, a positive consequence of coming to terms with a negative reality – that of living in and creating music in a discriminatory society. As Duke Ellington commented, 'There are [only] two kinds of music. Good music, and the other kind.'

These linguistic and politically motivated jazz wars were fought on the battlegrounds of the civil rights movement. Even before the radicalisation of jazz in the 1960s, an attitude and righteousness in jazz music ran parallel to collective African-American civil protest. So while this book is focussed primarily on the 1960s (and into the early 1970s), first we must briefly step back a few years further to understand the uninterrupted path of righteous black jazz.

Much as the arrival of bebop signalled the demise of swing during the second world war era, hard bop arrived in the mid-1950s, superseding cool jazz to reassert once again that jazz was primarily an African-American art form. Cool jazz, based on the west coast (far away from New York, the traditional epicentre of the jazz scene), mixed light jazz with 'sophisticated' harmonies and made musical links with European classical music and Brazilian bossa nova.

The only really important African-American artist in this style had been Miles Davis, and for the most part cool jazz was played by white musicians. When Davis subsequently formed his Quintet in 1955 (which included John Coltrane) he returned back to the musical structure of the blues, in so doing heralding the arrival of a new school of jazz – hard bop. One of the main proponents of this new style was Art Blakey and Horace Silver's super-tight, sharp-suited unit The Jazz Messengers, which through the 1950s and 1960s would feature many young future rising solo stars including Wayne Shorter, Lee Morgan and Donald Byrd. Hard bop was an extension of bebop without its complexities, returning the structure of jazz to its roots and adding the all-important new ingredients of rhythm and blues and gospel. In essence, it undeniably returned jazz music to its 'blackness'. If anything, hard bop was as radical a statement of blackness as free jazz or Afro-centricity would become in the next decade.

Three figures who radically altered the course of jazz music in the 1960s - Ornette Coleman, John Coltrane (top) and Miles Davis (right).

Volunteer civil right activists undergo tolerance training in preparation for 'sit-in' demonstrations, Petersburg, Virginia, May 1960. Here, NAACP student advisor David Gunter (left) and Leroy Hill (right) blow smoke into the face of Virginius Thornton.

Three forms of non-violent direct action and protest: View through the window of the 'Colored Waiting Room' of Freedom Riders as they wait in a bus station, Montgomery, Alabama, May 1961. The Freedom Riders rode buses throughout the southern United States in the months following the Boynton v. Virginia Supreme Court case, which essentially outlawed racial segregation on public transportation, in order to test and call attention to still existing local policies that ran contrary to national laws.

One of many sit-down demonstrations at a lunch counter in order to force integration.

The righteousness of hard bop was often expressed in song titles such as Horace Silver's The Preacher (Blue Note, 1955), Don Wilkerson's Preach Brother (Blue Note, 1962) and Jimmy Smith's The Sermon (Blue Note, 1962) and so on.

That this redefining or entrenchment of jazz music as distinctly African-American coincided with the rise of the civil rights movement was no coincidence. Similar themes such as a growing interest in Africa and its links with African-American culture were fuelled by a succession of African states becoming liberated during this era (17 African nations became independent in 1960). Notable albums at around this time include Art Blakey's African Beat (Blue Note, 1962), Randy Weston's Uhuru Africa (Roulette Records, 1962) and Music From The New African Nations (Colpix 1963).

By 1960, this righteousness had also become overtly political with Max Roach's groundbreaking We Insist - Freedom Now Suite (Candid, 1960) – whose cover featured three African-American men sitting at a 'whites only' lunch counter.

No matter how apolitical an artist may have been musically, if they had ever toured the South, slept in 'blacks only' hotels, played to segregated audiences, been a member of a separate musicians' union, swum in a segregated swimming pool, drunk from a 'colored only' water fountain, been denied entry to a restaurant, told to use a separate door, sit at a different table or go to the back of a bus, then civil rights was a fact of life for all African-American jazz musicians. It was as much a reality for an 'entertainer' such as organist Jimmy Smith as for a political radical such as Archie Shepp or the intergalactic Sun Ra.

Culture, especially music – and especially jazz – became of pivotal importance in the emancipation of African-Americans, and this correlation would only increase as the 1960s progressed.

The civil rights movement's main aim was to end racial segregation and discrimination and to enforce statutory voting rights for African-Americans. In 1954, the slow process of dismantling racist 'Jim Crow' laws began. State-sponsored school segregation was declared unconstitutional after the National Association for the Advancement of Colored People (NAACP)-sponsored Brown v Board of Education supreme court case, whose judgement overturned the long-standing Plessy v Ferguson court ruling of 1896 which had upheld the constitutionality of state laws requiring racial segregation in public facilities under the doctrine of 'separate but equal.'

While this new ruling was historic, the speed at which it was enforced was slow. And while the government attempted to enforce the dismantling of segregation in schools and public spaces, many southern states opposed the bill and fought its implementation. Thus began more than a decade of civil protests, from Rosa Parks and the Montgomery bus boycott to lunch-counter sit-ins and the freedom riders. African-Americans would have to wait until the 1964 Civil Rights Bill (which banned discrimination based on 'race, colour, religion, or national origin' in employment practices and public accommodations) and the Voting Rights Act of 1965 (protecting voting rights) to have all remnants of Jim Crow laws removed. For this there was also a heavy price to pay, including the assassinations of Malcolm X in 1965 and Martin Luther King in 1968.

In 1956, partly as a response to the growing civil rights movement but more significantly as a calculated countermove in the cold war political chess game, the American government initiated a diplomatic programme that engaged notable jazz musicians to act as goodwill envoys for their country, travelling and performing across far-flung regions of the world. State policy makers (correctly) understood that jazz was perceived as a culturally significant art form unique to America, and was therefore a symbolic representation of the values of the land of the free. These chosen 'jazz ambassadors', including Dizzy Gillespie, Louis Armstrong and Duke Ellington, were asked to promote and convey to host countries the core values of America – primarily the notion of 'freedom' - through their role as musicians.

This diplomatic manoeuvre was in response to the increasingly hostile cold war rhetoric of communism. Government sponsorship and recruitment of music and the co-opting of cultural identity was neither new nor unique to America. In the 1930s, for instance, Brazilian dictator Getúlio Vargas drew upon the music and culture of samba, manipulating its identity through a policy of state intervention and propaganda from an Afro-Brazilian art form into the defining national Brazilian music. In Jamaica in the early 1970s, Michael Manley used the language and imagery of the Rastafari faith (including charged rhetoric such as 'the Rod of Correction' and 'the land of sufferahs') in order to gain supporters for his 1972 election. In Germany in the 1940s, by contrast, the Nazi regime pronounced jazz music as degenerate, inferior to 'high German culture', and banned the broadcasting of jazz on German radio. This was partly because of its African roots and partly because many of the musicians who played jazz in Germany were of Jewish origin. In the cold war this fact became a useful tool for proclaiming America as free – and jazz a weapon of that freedom.

Demonstrators picket in front of a school board office in protest against segregation, St Louis, Missouri, early 1960s.

View of segregated public toilets labelled 'ladies', 'men' and 'colored', circa 1960.

Albany Standoff: American law enforcement officer Police Chief Laurie Pritchett speaking with Civil Rights leader Reverend Martin Luther King Jr and Dr William G. Anderson during anti-segregation demonstration, Albany, Georgia, July 1962.

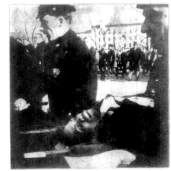

The deep irony of the elevation of jazz musicians to the status of national heroes was that whilst African-American musicians were chosen to act as envoys of freedom abroad, at home they were still treated as second-class citizens. This irony was not lost to the jazz musicians involved, and the schizophrenic pressure on Gillespie, Armstrong and Ellington and others who took part in this extravagant diplomatic gesture became just one more example of the hypocrisy and bigotry that was a part of daily life for African-Americans and from which they were expected to rise above.

'Jazz ambassador' Duke Ellington, for instance, suffered the ignominy of being the first jazz musician to be nominated for the Pulitzer prize for music in 1965 – only to be told that the board had refused to recognise Ellington, and that no prize would be given that year. In fact it would be 31 years before Wynton Marsalis became the first jazz musician to win this award. It was 25 years after Ellington's death when he was posthumously given the award in 1999.

Incidents such as this were hardly uncommon. Nina Simone said the driving force to her career was her rejection from the classical music conservatory the Curtis Institute of Music, which she believed denied her the opportunity to have become the first black student accepted for classical music.

Miles Davis, after being beaten up by policemen outside a nightclub, eventually dropped his lawsuit against New York City's police in a plea bargain to recover his suspended cabaret card. This card was a necessary bureaucratic device to performing live – and entertainers were automatically deprived of them if awaiting a trial. Davis wrote that the incident 'changed my whole life and whole attitude again, made me feel bitter and cynical again when I was starting to feel good about the things that had changed in this country'.

And buried deep beneath all of Sun Ra's playful, Afro-futurist metaphysics, Ra-history and science fiction was the profound and utter sense of alienation that he felt living in a society that discriminates on the colour of someone's skin. No, the hypocrisy of the US government was simply a part of the everyday tension of creative life for all African-American artists.

In 1960, Ornette Coleman not only released This is our Music, but also Free Jazz: A Collective Improvisation. This pivotal release marked the start of the free jazz movement. The new radical developments of Coleman as well as John Coltrane and Cecil Taylor during this period liberated jazz artists from the previous restrictions of chords, scales and time signatures, enabling them to explore further the outer, often existential regions of expression, of the soul.

What was so powerful and revolutionary about free jazz was that this musical freeing from tradition coincided philosophically with and mirrored the everyday liberation aims of the civil rights movement. The collective improvisation of this new music enabled a musical language that could, if it wished to, emulate the scream and horror of pain. As Archie Shepp commented,

> 'Music must at times terrify! It must shake men by the throats! … Sometimes we must bludgeon beauty to seeming death; make it ugly; simply because life itself is at times ugly and painful to behold.'

As this expression became more extreme, in the process it often alienated audiences (after all, 'alienation' was often the subject matter). Many indignant and bemused (white) critics accused the music of being too European-based, of losing its African-American root, and of moving instead towards the new European modernism of Cage, Webern and Schoenberg. It was no such thing. African-American jazz musicians – to return to the example of Brazilian culture again for a moment – were, in a fashion similar to the Tropicália artists of the late 1960s, engaging in the 'anthropophagy' of European culture – eating it up and digesting it in order to enhance their own music.

The photograph of Ornette Coleman taken at the beginning of the decade (page 43) offers us a rare and beautiful smile – one of the few you will see in the book. Ornette is relaxed and at ease at the time of his New York debut. Little sign is there in this picture of the revolutionary chaos that his music was about to unleash on America – discordant, radical and perplexing.

Barely two years later Coleman would simply stop performing live for three years – in frustration at the nightclubs, critics, musicians and audience who failed to see or understand clearly his vision. His vision was so profound that it would have to wait until the dismantling of the institutions of jazz (as the music moved from nightclub to art space, from entertainment to artistry) – mirroring the destruction of the traditional musical building blocks of jazz – before it could make real sense.

But here, for now, Ornette is happy. Only he knows the challenges he is about to take on, and he is prepared. Young (unencumbered by the past), smart but also relaxed (white collar and tie hidden beneath his jumper), he adopts a traditional jazz musicians' studio pose while subverting it with his white saxophone, one which had recently replaced his trademark 'inauthentic' plastic horn. Perhaps he realises that 50 years on his steadfast adherence to principles would make him a national icon, lifetime Grammy awardée, Pulitzer prize winner and honorary doctor of music.

Young paper boy during the March on Washington for Jobs and Freedom political rally held in Washington, DC on August 28, 1963. The event was one of the largest political rallies for human rights in United States history and called for civil and economic rights for African-Americans.

Running parallel to the civil rights movement, African-American jazz musicians became increasingly interested in both the music and heritage of Africa, following the liberation of African states. Two pioneering jazz artists in this context were Art Blakey (main) and Yusef Lateef (top right). Patrice Lumumba (bottom right) was the first democratically elected Prime Minister of the Republic of Congo in 1960. His execution the following year implicated the United States (via the CIA), Britain (via MI6) and Belgium.

If Coleman was the first radical in this revolutionary decade, John Coltrane was to prove to be the most significant force in jazz music in the 1960s up until and beyond his death in 1967. For critics and fans who saw in the free jazz avant-gardists of the day an absolving of blackness, a leaning towards European art music rather than African-American, in Coltrane no such charge could be made. One of the reasons for this was that Coltrane, unlike his free jazz compatriots, already had history. His stint playing in the Miles Davis Quintet had culminated in the 1959 album Kind of Blue – in many ways as radical a piece of music as Ornette Coleman's releases a year later. On this album Davis used modal scales, a theoretical slight of hand, which first freed the musicians from using the endless established chord changes of bebop. That he managed this while also celebrating the original African-American art-form – blues – signified a music that was both avant-garde and black.

When Coltrane left Davis's group in 1960 to launch his own, signing first with Atlantic Records and then most significantly with Impulse! Records, in this seven-year period he produced an intense, profound, lyrical and forward-thinking body of work - a creative output unmatched by any artist during this time, or ever since.

Coltrane was uniquely capable of connecting African-American consciousness with the avant-garde, his progressive musical ideas perhaps best exemplified by a song such as Alabama, written in response to the bombing by the Ku Klux Klan of the 16th Street Baptist Church in Birmingham, Alabama on September 15, 1963 – an attack that killed four young girls, Addie Mae Collins, Denise McNair, Carole Robertson and Cynthia Wesley. Wordlessly, Coltrane based the melody to the song on the syntax and flow of Martin Luther King's eulogy at the children's funeral.

In 1965 his seminal work, A Love Supreme, brought a previously unseen spirituality to the new music, centred around his poem to an all-denominational god, allegedly written by Coltrane after an epiphany experienced after coming off heroin addiction at the end of the 1950s (a common consequence and fact of jazz life for many in the 1950s).

Of this spirituality Coltrane wrote:

> 'My goal is to live the truly religious life, and express it in my music. If you live it, when you play there's no problem because the music is part of the whole thing. To be a musician is really something. It goes very, very deep. My music is the spiritual expression of what I am – my faith, my knowledge, my being.'

After 1965 Coltrane continued his work performing and recording with many of the new generation of free jazz and 'new thing' artists including Pharoah Sanders, Alice Coltrane (his second wife), Rashied Ali, Marion Brown and Archie Shepp, giving legitimacy to their radical music and pushing his own to even more further extremes. He imbued previously unheard of levels of integrity, spirituality, self-pride and worth for African-American jazz musicians. For a most apolitical commentator Coltrane's life and music was perhaps the most political of all.

By the mid-1960s the politicisation of jazz had become more overt following the death of Malcolm X, the birth of the Black Panthers, and the rise of the Black Power movement, as self-determination, self-empowerment and pride became key aspects of creative integrity. Amiri Baraka's highly politicised Black Arts Movement called for more strident African-American art in all forms and gave rise to a pronounced Afro-centricity in jazz.

Afro-centricity became an important concept for jazz musicians, a continued looking towards Africa as both musical source and cultural history. This exploration, alongside the concepts of collective improvisation earlier developed by Coleman and Coltrane, helped inspire the establishment of African-American musical collectives. The best known of these (and still running) was the Association for the Advancement of Creative Musicians, founded in Chicago in 1965.

This organisation came out of composer and pianist Muhal Richard Abrams' earlier collective Experimental Band, a large group line-up that began rehearsing on the south side of Chicago, strikingly captured here in the 1960s (page 70 and elsewhere) in a number of stunning, rarely-seen photographs by Chicago Defender photographer Robert Abbott Sengstacke. Sengstacke was the son of newspaper publisher John H Sengstacke, and described by the New York Times as 'one of the most significant photographers of the civil rights generation'. He began documenting the AACM 50 years ago and has been photographing them ever since. In these photographs you will see all the future members of the Art Ensemble of Chicago – Lester Bowie, Joseph Jarman and Roscoe Mitchell – as well as association members Phil Cohran, Anthony Braxton and Leroy Jenkins.

Other collectives that formed around this time included the Black Artists Group based in St Louis (whose members included Oliver Lake, Julius Hemphill and Hamiet Bluiett); the Jazz Composers Guild in New York (founded by Bill Dixon); and the Underground Musicians Association (UGMA), – which later changed its name to the Union of God's Musicians and Artists Ascension (UGMAA) – in Los Angeles (founded by Horace Tapscott). Aside from their collective improvisation, these groups made significant connections with all aspects of avant-garde art, including dance, theatre and poetry, as well as establishing and strengthening local community links through performance and education. To a certain extent these collectives also took on the responsibility of teaching black musical history, a role previously carried out by the (now defunct) segregated black musicians' unions.

The 16th Street Baptist Church in Birmingham, Alabama was bombed on Sunday, September 15, 1963, killing four African-American girls - Addie Mae Collins (age 14), Denise McNair (age 11), Carole Robertson (age 14), and Cynthia Wesley (age 14). Civil rights leaders Martin Luther King (third from right), Ralph Abernathy (holding paper) and Fred Shuttlesworth in clerical robes after the funeral. John Coltrane wrote the song 'Alabama' in response to the bombings, the melody based on the intonation of King's soliloquy at the funeral.

Young boys jump over a puddle while playing on the streets of a Southside Chicago neighbourhood, circa 1965. In the 1960s Southside Chicago gave rise to the experimental groups and collectives of Muhal Richard Abrams' Experimental Band, The Association for the Advancement of Creative Musicians, Phil Cohran's Artistic Heritage Ensemble and The Art Ensemble of Chicago.

Another interesting aspect of jazz in the 1960s is that while this revolutionary, free and Afro-centric jazz was endlessly discussed and debated in print, the many pioneering and radical artists from earlier eras in jazz were of course still making their own music, and were often as forward-thinking as the relative newcomers.

Those powerhouse inventors of bebop back in the 1940s and hard bop in the 1950s – including Miles Davis, Dizzy Gillespie, Thelonious Monk, Art Blakey, Charlie Mingus, Max Roach – were all adding to the scene in the 1960s. There were the towering musical figureheads of Duke Ellington and Louis Armstrong. An artist such as pianist and composer Mary Lou Williams (arranger for Ellington in the 1940s and mentor to Charlie Parker and Thelonious Monk) was to make some of her most profound music in the 1960s (such as Black Christ of The Andes, Folkways 1964).

And while Coltrane may have taken the baton from his band leader Miles Davis at the start of the 1960s (as Davis himself had done after his time with Charlie Parker), it would be foolish to dismiss the radicals of previous eras as has-beens; by the end of the decade it was Miles Davis's pioneering electric rock experiments that would lead to further radical changes in jazz heading into the 1970s.

Similarly the most important groups of the 1950s gave rise in the 1960s to successful solo careers, groups such as The Jazz Messengers helped launch Horace Silver, Art Blakey, Lee Morgan and Donald Byrd. As well as Miles Davis and John Coltrane, Davis's legendary Quintet also included Cannonball Adderley, who along with his brother Nat, found huge commercial success, bringing the world of hard bop closer to rhythm and blues with their pioneering sound of soul jazz.

Soul jazz found favour with African-Americans audiences who sometimes felt disengaged from free jazz. Soul music was ying to the yang of jazz, two sides of the same coin. Their union was rarely appreciated by critics and purists alike, but was most definitely a hit with African-American audiences, a fact certainly not lost at Atlantic Records which in the 1960s promoted (and sold) the soul music of Aretha Franklin, Otis Redding and Wilson Pickett alongside jazz artists such as Dave Newman, Hubert Laws, Charles Lloyd and Roy Ayers. Many of these jazz artists were also hard working session players and regularly performed on countless Atlantic soul sessions.

Unlike free jazz, soul jazz artists kept to the same constant beat as rhythm and blues. This to an extent coincided with the Afro-centric exploration of polyrhythms within the parallel universe of the militant nationalists of free jazz, making the musical distinction between 'commercial' and 'uncommercial' jazz artists in some ways less straightforward than at the start of the decade. After all, the polemical discord between revolutionary and entertainer was more complex than at first glance – with 'commercial' artists such as Roland Kirk or Yusef Lateef (both signed to Atlantic in the late 1960s) more than capable of their own radical experimentalism.* Conversely, even the supreme revolutionary John Coltrane recorded an album of jazz standards with vocalist Johnny Hartman the same year that he made his groundbreaking Impressions (1963).

In point of fact, by the end of the 1960s many of the artists involved in free experimentation and the avant-garde had either migrated to, or spent much of their time in, Europe. Artists such as the Art Ensemble of Chicago, Anthony Braxton, Don Cherry, Sunny Murray, the Black Artists Group and Archie Shepp found themselves living abroad in societies that were, on the surface at least, less overtly racist to African-Americans than back in the States. And they were playing to new audiences who were refreshingly receptive to their groundbreaking ideas.

In 1969, Bob Thiele, who had so successfully produced John Coltrane and other radical artists at Impulse Records (including Archie Shepp, Pharoah Sanders and Alice Coltrane), left the company to found a new label, Flying Dutchman. Here Thiele successfully worked with a new generation of younger artists – including poet Gil Scott-Heron, vocalist Leon Thomas and keyboardist Lonnie Liston Smith – all of whom were making music that furthered the spiritual and exploratory aspects of the work of John Coltrane and the other radical free jazz artists of the 1960s but with an accessibility lacking in many earlier generation free artists.

At the start of the 1970s, perhaps partly as a consequence of the exodus of free jazz musicians to Europe, 'commercial' jazz artists in America – labelled crossover, soul jazz or fusion artists – unexpectedly found themselves in a position where they were able to make, perhaps ironically, some of the most progressive music of the era. Independent jazz record labels such as Blue Note, Milestone and Prestige gave musicians the freedom to stretch themselves outside the sometimes restrictive limitations of producing 'commercially viable' jazz music in the 1960s (which had often involved a lack of rehearsal time before recording dates, keeping to a familiar formula, and so on).

An artist such as Cannonball Adderley, for example, who had begun his career back in 1955 with Miles Davis, created some of the most experimental work of his career in the early 1970s working alongside producer David Axelrod with work such as Soul of the Bible (Capitol, 1972) and Soul Zodiac (Capitol, 1972). Similarly Horace Silver, one of the originators of hard bop in the 1950s, explored a spiritual and vocal stretching-out for Blue Note in the late 1960s to create some of his most progressive music of his career (You Got To Take A Little Love, 1969; Total Response, 1970; That Healin' Feelin', 1970; and All, 1972).

Art Blakey and Horace Silver's Jazz Messengers pioneered the sound of hard bop with their early releases on the Blue Note label. Here we see Art Blakey, Walt Harper, Horace Silver, Jon Morris, Skeets Talbot, Earl Mays, and Hank Mobley, on Walt Harper's radio show at WHOD radio station studio, Pittsburgh, Pennsylvania, July 1955.

Cover of a booklet prepared by the student movement praising the Black Power Movement, USA, 1967

Black Panthers Protest At NYC Courthouse. View of a line of Black Panther Party members as they stand outside the New York City courthouse under a portion of an Abraham Lincoln quote which reads 'The Ultimate Justice of the People,' New York, New York, April 11, 1969.

LeRoi Jones (Amiri Baraka) started the Black Arts Movement, which aligned African-American arts to the Black Power Movement.

Much of the new freedom given to these artists was possible because of the commercial success that Miles Davis had achieved with his creative exploration and fusion of the previously separate musical worlds of jazz and rock. Davis opened up a whole new audience for jazz musicians. By 1973 an artist such as Herbie Hancock, former pianist in the Miles Davis Quintet from 1963 to 1968 and a successful solo artist on Blue Note Records in the 1960s, became the first jazz artist to sell a million records with the release of Headhunters (Colombia, 1973) which explored a radical fusion of electronic jazz and funk aesthetic at the same time as becoming one of the most commercially successful jazz albums of the era. Other 'fusion' artists such as Donald Byrd (who started his career playing bop in the Jazz Messengers back in 1955), Stanley Clarke and George Duke also found great success in the 1970s making music that combined commercial accessibility with progressive, forward-looking music.

To the linear mind – be it academic, journalistic or recreational - the proliferation of styles and breaking-up of the accepted rule book of jazz in the 1960s and into the 1970s was often dismissed as a mass of noisy in-fighting after the hegemony of traditional jazz, swing and even bebop. But for most of those making the music, all was clear and in focus, their senses sharpened by the reality that 400 years of oppression were drawing to a close.

Like music, photography circumvents the need for language, for words. As journalists and critics eloquently try and fail to analyse, pontificate, judge, criticise, comment and explain the meaning of it all, the photograph expresses complex emotions and meanings wordlessly.

Perhaps the most striking aspect of the photographs in this book is that one theme dominates all the imagery - the all-encompassing self-awareness of the artists – a self-determination so apparent in how they choose to present themselves to the camera.

Sartorially we see a variety of styles through the book. The cosmic/outer-world/African chic of nationalism contrasts strongly with the suited-and-booted hard bop/soul jazz style, first seen in the 1950s with Jazz Messengers – Art Blakey, Lee Morgan, Wayne Shorter. The look of hard bop was as tailored as the 'cool' period Miles Davis – hip, sharp and getting down to business. In fact, by the end of the 1960s the at-all-times-studied style of Miles Davis himself had become otherworldly (see, for instance, page 90) as his music similarly entered new frontiers.

All the revolutionary jazz musicians captured here are in the constant process of redefining themselves as artists. Their eyes, like their music, belie deeply intense and complex emotions that carry the weight. But, as already noted, most apparent is the overwhelming look of self-confidence.

By the dawn of the 1960s the ingratiating 'Uncle Tom' smile of first generation black entertainers was long gone. The foundation jazz artist (and jazz ambassador) Louis Armstrong was sometimes referred to disparagingly as such on account of his ever-present smiling demeanour in photographs. But Armstrong himself could, on occasion, subvert this image, signifyin' on the implied (to some) subservience of this smile. One example was in 1957, when Armstrong used his high profile to publicly express his opposition to the Arkansas state governor's decision to ban African-American students in Little Rock from entering a newly desegregated white public school. On President Dwight Eisenhower's refusal to intervene in the matter, Armstrong declared: 'The way they are treating my people in the South, the government can go to hell.'

Armstrong's intervention was doubly powerful because he had previously declared himself apolitical: 'I don't get involved in politics, I just blow my horn.' He accused Eisenhower of being two-faced and gutless: 'It's getting almost so bad, a coloured man hasn't got any country … The people over there [abroad] ask me what's wrong with my country. What am I supposed to say?'

And it was the president, and not Armstrong, who later rescinded when he sent 1,200 paratroopers in to Arkansas to ensure that the Little Rock Nine African-American students could enter school.

By the start of the 1970s jazz had come a long way from its roots in Storyville, New Orleans. Free and radical jazz entered Europe, as well as the American academic world and later the loft spaces of New York, always in search of an appropriate and suitable setting for its righteously indignant non-commercialism. Soul jazz and fusion, in contrast, reached stunning new heights of commercial success.

Featured here are the many figures who shaped and influenced jazz throughout the 1960s, that most revolutionary of eras, and onwards into the 1970s.

Stuart Baker

*Examples of Roland Kirk's experimentalism might include The Case of the Three Sided Dream (a double album with one whole side devoted to recorded 'silence' in the studio). For Lateef, try In A Little Spanish Town on the album The Doctor Is In, on which Yusef plays along to a 1926 gramophone recording of a song written by Mabel Wayne.

Little Rock, Arkansas, 1957. National Guardsmen, having admitted white children to a school, bar the way to a black student. The Guardsmen came under the authority of local pro-segregationist governor Orval Faubus. President Eisenhower initially did not intervene, leading the usually apolitical 'jazz ambassador' Louis Armstrong to speak out in protest. Eisenhower eventually sent in the army and federalised the Guardsmen (so that they came under government control, see photo at right) in order to enforce integration at Little Rock Central High for the first nine African-American children admitted.

BLACK FIRE! NEW SPIRITS!

IMAGES OF A REVOLUTION RADICAL JAZZ IN THE USA 1960-75

Herbie Hancock

Born in Chicago in 1940, keyboardist and composer Herbie Hancock has managed to segue, Zelig-like, into each evolving era of black music, often composing an era's defining musical example. Classically trained, his success lies partly in rendering complex music easily accessible, without sacrificing quality or creativity. He joined Miles Davis' second great quintet in 1963 and also cut a string of classic albums for Blue Note, including 'Maiden Voyage' (1965) and 'The Prisoner' (1969). A stint at Warners followed, where he pursued a more ethereal musical path, laced with analog synths. After a while he was 'missing Earth', as he put it, which resulted in the hugely successful 'Headhunters' (Columbia 1973) that featured jazz improvisation over the heaviest of grooves on tracks like 'Chameleon'. He continued in a similar vein on 'Thrust' (Columbia 1974), 'Secrets' (Columbia 1976) and the astonishing live recording 'Flood' (CBS/Sony 1975). He caught the trend of the times again with his hit 'I Thought It Was You', and in the early 80s 'Rockit' was, for many people, their first taste of nascent hip-hop and became the first black music video to be played on the then new MTV. He continually performs and records today, switching between genres with ease. Ever the innovator, his most recent solo show saw him utilising several iPads at once to create interpretations of his best known tracks.

Elvin Jones

Born in 1927 in Detroit, Jones moved to New York in 1955 after serving in the army. He played with Bud Powell and Charles Mingus, but is most readily associated with John Coltrane. With his sharp, powerful and polyrhythmic style, he found a perfect foil in Coltrane, who could easily absorb and play off of his rhythmic assaults.

Jones had previously played with Miles Davis in 1958, and a year after he featured on 'A Night at The Village Vanguard' with Sonny Rollins. He became part of Coltrane's group proper in 1960, cutting classics including 'My Favorite Things' (Atlantic 1960) 'Impressions' (Impulse! 1963), and of course 'A Love Supreme' (Impulse! 1964).

The addition of a second drummer to Coltrane's group in 1965, Rashied Ali, saw Jones' exit soon after, whereupon he embarked on a successful solo and band-leading career, releasing several albums on Blue Note, Impulse! & Vanguard. He passed away in 2004 from heart failure.

Nina Simone

Born in 1933, Nina Simone drew on her classical background, as well as jazz and blues, in her vocal and piano playing style. Her approach shifted in the 1960s as she became a vocal supporter of the civil rights movement, evident in the explicit 'Mississippi Goddam', as well as her adoption of other songs, which she then imbued with her own meaning and gravitas, such as 'To Be Young, Gifted and Black'. In addition to this, she would reference her African heritage in tracks like 'Zungo', 'See-Line Woman' and 'African Mailman'. Long periods of traveling between countries lessened her recording and live work in later years, though she would perform until her passing in 2003.

Pharoah Sanders

The radical avenues that jazz explored from the mid-60s onwards were given context by the social and political changes during this turbulent period. While one didn't necessarily give birth to the other, as jazz had risen on a sharp creative curve from the 1940s onwards, the two correlated during one of the most significant modern shifts in American life. One player who exemplified this wave was Pharoah Sanders. His often anguished playing appeared to give voice to powerful emotions, and the themes of his compositions would hint at political subtexts, without always being explicit.

Born Farrell Sanders in 1940, he moved to New York in 1960, having studied and played music from a young age. His early experience in the city was difficult and he would often sleep rough. Initially looked after by Sun Ra, he eventually came to John Coltrane's attention and became a regular fixture in his group from 1964, which lead to a natural affiliation with Impulse! The label released some of Sanders' finest work like Thembi (1971), Black Unity (1971) and Karma (1969), which featured the celebrated 'The Creator Has A Master Plan' with vocalist Leon Thomas. During this period he also worked with Alice Coltrane. He still performs regularly today.

Elvin Jones

Don Moye

Whilst best known for his work with The Art Ensemble of Chicago, Famadou Don Moye also has a history of percussion work with musicians like Sonny Sharrock and Pharoah Sanders, and was already playing in Paris prior to the The Art Ensemble's arrival at the end of the 1960s. He joined the group in Europe, recording and performing live with them, before returning to America in 1971. He has also worked with Randy Weston and Steve McCall. In the 1980s he formed a 'super group', 'The Leaders', with Lester Bowie, Arthur Blythe and other avant-garde luminaries. He recorded as leader on 'Sun Percussion Vol 1.' (AECO 1975) as well as with various AACM members, and still performs today.

Roland Kirk

Rahsaan Roland Kirk was one of America's truly unique artists. Although he was sometimes derided as 'eccentric' for his polemical statements in between songs, or his 'gimmick' of playing three saxophones at once, this detracts from Kirk's astounding technique (he used, for instance, circular breathing from the 1960s onwards) and his vast musical knowledge which he would at times reference in his compositions. Despite being blind from the age of two, he became a prolific bandleader and player, recording a number of startling albums for Atlantic Records including 'The Inflated Tear' (1967) and 'Volunteered Slavery' (1969). His career was sadly brought to an end by a stroke in 1976.

Albert Ayler

Born in 1936, Ayler is one of the most regularly cited but often misunderstood pioneers in jazz music. Known for his harsh and often wailing tone as a saxophonist, Ayler's playing reflected myriad elements from across America's musical canon. Dirges, fiery R&B, and spirituals seep through his playing, in a too short career tragically cut short by a suspected suicide in 1970.

After a stint in the army, Ayler relocated to Europe where his developing, idiosyncratic style found an audience, and he cut 'My Name Is Albert Ayler' (Debut) with local musicians in Denmark in 1964. After returning to America, Ayler recorded seminal material for ESP-Disk, alongside Gary Peacock and Sunny Murray, such as 'Spiritual Unity' (1964) and 'Spirits Rejoice' (1965). John Coltrane was a fan of Ayler's work, and helped him secure a deal with Impulse! for whom he cut his final studio recordings prior to his death.

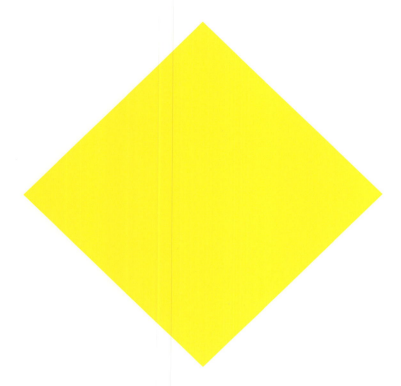

Ornette Coleman

Ornette Coleman is possibly the most controversial, as well as influential musician, featured in this book. In addition to his skills as a composer and saxophonist he pioneered the concept of deconstructing the basic norms of melody and harmony. Although termed 'Free Jazz', his music was based on pushing the boundaries of pre-determined composition, as opposed to just improvisation.

Born into rural poverty in Fort Worth, Texas in 1930, he was playing saxophone professionally from his early teens. By the end of the 1950s he was working with a core quartet of Don Cherry, Billy Higgins and Charlie Haden, and recording for Contemporary and then Atlantic on LPs such as 'The Shape of Jazz to Come' (1959) and 'Ornette' (1961). While in New York, Coleman's playing caught the attention of John Coltrane and Albert Ayler, both of whom drew inspiration from this radical new approach to form. Later in the decade he would record for Blue Note and Impulse!, and his ideas seemed less outlandish in the context of the developing avant-garde, which in time would hail him as its boldest forerunner.

The Art Ensemble of Chicago

Nurtured in the creative environment of Chicago's Association for the Advancement of Creative Musicians, The Art Ensemble of Chicago came together in the late 1960s. Playing music with their focus firmly on the future, the group's multi-instrumental approach reflected the history of jazz, including its foundation in the blues.

The band consisted of five core musicians, Lester Bowie on trumpet, Malachi Favors on bass, and Roscoe Mitchell and Joseph Jarman both on saxophone. Drummer Philip Wilson was replaced by Famoudou Don Moye, who played percussion as well as drums.

Whilst active in their native city, it wasn't until the band relocated to France that they started to receive recognition. There they recorded their now signature 'Theme De YoYo' as part of the 'Les Stances a Sophie' soundtrack (EMI Pathé/Nessa 1970). Returning to America they recorded two titles for Atlantic 'Bap-Tizum' (1972) and 'Fanfare For The Warriors' (1973), as well as various solo projects. Despite the passing of Bowie and Favors, the surviving members still sporadically work together, keeping alive their motto, 'Great Black Music: Ancient to the Future.'

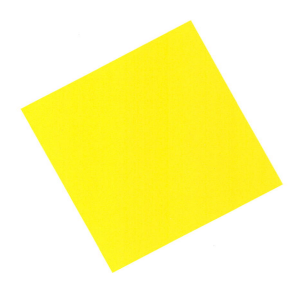

Alice Coltrane

Born Alice Mcleod in 1937 in Detroit, Coltrane graduated from The Detroit Institute of Technology, having completed her studies in classical music, and began playing the piano and organ regularly in public, often in church.

She moved to New York in 1962, meeting John Coltrane while she was playing in Terry Gibbs' quartet, and they married in 1965. In 1966, she became part of his evolving quintet, (replacing McCoy Tyner) as well as raising their family.

When John died in 1967, she came into her own as a solo artist, mastering the harp her husband had bought her prior to his passing, and went on to have a successful career as a band leader and composer. Beginning with 'A Monastic Trio' in 1967, her best solo outings continued on a similar spiritual plane to her late husband, and albums such as 'Journey In Satchidananda' (Impulse! 1970) and 'World Galaxy' (Impulse! 1972), are characterised by dense bass drones, offset by her shimmering harp or keyboard work. She continued to record and perform live until her passing in 2007.

Archie Shepp

One of the most politically overt musicians of his peers, Sheep can seemingly castigate the audience with his saxophone. Born in 1937, he initially worked with Cecil Taylor, Don Cherry and Bill Dixon, before coming to the attention of John Coltrane. They took a side each of the 'New Thing at Newport' LP (Impulse! 1965), and Shepp also contributed to the 'A Love Supreme' sessions. Shepp then recorded for Impulse! and albums like 'Fire Music' (Impulse! 1965) exemplified Shepp's internal political shifts that peaked with the monumental 'Attica Blues' (Impulse! 1972), an album in the protest tradition that explored the aftermath of the prison riots of the title. Even when not as politically direct as the latter, his music was always shot through with a radical spirit, like 'Yasmina, A Black Woman' (BYG-Actuel 1969) and 'Force: Sweet Mao - Suid Africa '76' (Uniteledis 1976) a duet with Max Roach. Shepp has consistently explored African-American music traditions throughout his career, whilst maintaining a political stance that has not abated with age.

Yusef Lateef

Born in Chatanooga, Tennessee in 1920, Lateef (born William Huddleston) and his family moved to Detroit in 1925. Lateef's conversion to Islam coincided with an enduring change to his musical approach, and additionally dovetailed with his studies and research into African music forms.

His appropriation of eastern scales had a profound effect on John Coltrane amongst others, and in the late 1950s, and early 1960s he recorded 'Prayer To The East' and 'Eastern Sounds', on Savoy and Prestige respectively.

Taking part in Randy Weston's 'Uhuru Africa' project, brought Lateef into contact with percussionist Babatunde Olatunji, and the pair participated in Art Blakey's ground breaking 'The African Beat' (Blue Note 1962). What is striking about Lateef is his consistent commitment to his musical and intellectual vision. After recording numerous albums for Impulse! and Atlantic, he spent the first part of the 1980s working at the Center for Nigerian Cultural Studies in Zaria, North Nigeria which resulted in the album 'Yusef Lateef in Nigeria' (Landmark 1983).
In his nineties, Lateef continued to experiment with his own YAL label as well as work with the Go:Organic Orchestra alongside Adam Rudolph. He passed away aged 93 in 2013.

Pharoah Sanders

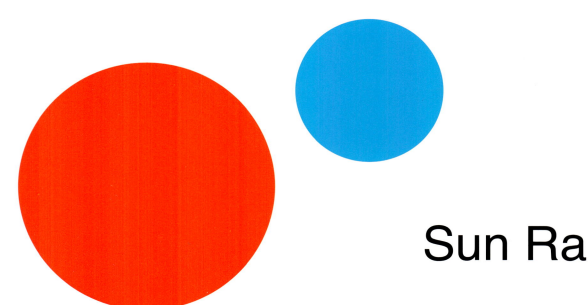

Sun Ra

Born Herman Poole Blount in Alabama in 1914, Sun Ra's influence as a composer, philosopher, and electronic music pioneer is probably incalculable. Although details are sparse regarding his childhood, he displayed prodigious musical talent from an early age, and was able to sight read and memorise complex pieces of music from his teenage years onwards. He worked first with local bands, but built a reputation for himself as a dedicated musician, focusing ever intently on composing and rehearsal. Having avoided the military draft in the early 1940s, Ra moved to Chicago, and in 1946 was hired by Fletcher Henderson, then in the twilight of his career, as a pianist and arranger. The social and political atmosphere of 1940s Chicago also started to radicalise and change Ra's outlook, and although the exact date remains in conjecture, it is in this period that Ra most likely experienced his out-of-body journey to Saturn that would prove so pivotal to his identity.

His time in Chicago continued to galvanise his creative output also, and he started to experiment with musicians like Pat Patrick, Marshall Allen and John Gilmore. Here he also met long time associate Alton Abraham with whom he set up El Saturn Records, an independent label which became an outlet for the myriad recordings Ra made, many of which took place at his home. The label's first release was in 1957.

His band, now known as The Arkestra, began performing regularly, wearing their celebrated outlandish stage gear that hinted at both outer space and ancient Egypt simultaneously. While their music was rooted in elements of bop and the big band tradition, it was Ra's inclusion of African instruments, modal elements, and strange harmonies that contributed to the unsettling and unique nature of the Arkestra's performances. After Chicago, the band, stranded in New York after a car accident, ended up staying there for most of the 1960s, where they played regularly at the avant-garde venue Slug's Saloon, in a period which saw a rising awareness of Ra and his ideas. The band would ultimately move to Philadelphia which, on and off would become Ra's, and the rotating membership of the Arkestra's, base. Ra would continue to write and rehearse daily, a seemingly endless fount of musical ideas.

What is remarkable and singular about Sun Ra and his associates, is how they embodied, challenged and progressed so many elements of the Afro-American experience. His compositions signified the 'new' music, blues, the history of jazz and even elements of the classical world, without necessarily aligning itself with any group or movement per se.

His promotion of black history and elements of African religion and mythology sought to counterbalance the Euro-centric status quo, and even the band's costumes undermined and pushed the patronising notion of minstrelsy to its most uncomfortable extreme. In addition to their own releases, some of Ra's recordings reached a wider audience through albums on ESP, Impulse! and the monumental 'Space Is The Place' on Blue Thumb. While they made many great records, it was the live arena that proved the truest place to experience Sun Ra and The Arkestra as artists and performers, and they toured the world over before Ra's passing in 1993. The Arkestra continue to play today, under the leadership of Marshall Allen.

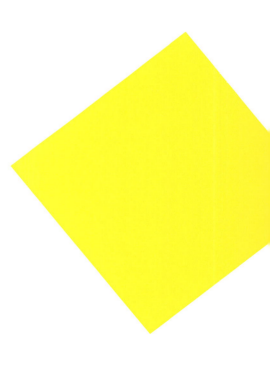

Mary Lou Williams

Mary Lou Williams embodies American jazz history, and her abilities and musical foresight don't receive nearly enough credit. A child prodigy, her astonishing career included arranging for Duke Ellington, mentoring Thelonious Monk and Dizzy Gillespie, as well as remarkable solo recordings like 'Black Christ of the Andes' (Folkways 1963). Born in 1910 in Atlanta her style evolved from vaudeville, through to big band jazz, bebop and beyond. She worked freelance, arranging for Benny Goodman and Tommy Dorsey, and a radio show and residency at Cafe Society in New York brought her into contact with Gillespie et al. A sojourn in Europe coincided with a conversion to Catholicism and a break from music, though she returned at the end of the 1950s to perform with Gillespie at the Newport Jazz Festival. She recorded for Decca, Columbia, Folkways and her own 'Mary' label, and latterly combined her faith with religiously inspired compositions such as 'Mary Lou's Mass' (Mary 1964) as well as charitable work helping fellow musicians. She was musically active until her passing in 1981.

Randy Weston

Pianist and composer Weston is one of the key musicians in 20th century music to explore in detail the many links between Afro-American music forms and their roots in the African continent. Born in Brooklyn in 1926, his Panamanian father imbued an interest and pride in their heritage that carried through into Weston's music. He would eventually relocate to Morocco, and North African strains can be heard in albums such as 'Blue Moses' (CTI 1972) and 'Tanjah' (Polydor 1973). From the 1950s onwards, his piano playing echoed rhythm and drumming techniques, some of which were gleaned from his father's record collection. An additional influence, which he mentions in Valerie Wilmer's excellent 'Jazz People', was the fact that one of his dad's restaurants in Brooklyn became a hang out for heavyweights such as Miles Davis, Dizzy Gillespie and Charlie Parker, and sometimes the conversations and socialising would continue after-hours at Weston's apartment.

As a player, Weston was also influenced by Thelonious Monk and Duke Ellington, the latter recording him for a personal label project that never came to fruition, although the resulting 'Berkshire Blues', eventually came out on Arista's Freedom label. At the turn of the 1960s Weston recorded three albums which fused African idioms alongside his jazz compositions, 'Highlife' (Colpix 1963), 'Randy' (Bakton 1964), later re-released on Atlantic as 'African Cookbook', and 'Uhuru Afrika' (Roulette 1960). The latter was an ambitious project with poet Langston Hughes, and included Gigi Gryce, Babatunde Olatunji and Melba Liston amongst a stellar line-up. The resulting visit to Nigeria in 1961 to perform the project live proved the first opportunity for Weston to consolidate his connection with Africa, which has characterised his music and life up to the present day.

Ron Carter

Born in 1937, double bassist Carter has played on over 2000 albums, during a prestigious career that has seen him work with many greats including Eric Dolphy, Herbie Hancock and Sam Rivers and record as a sideman and band leader, most notably for the Blue Note and CTI labels. From 1963 to 1968 he was part of Miles Davis' classic quintet, playing on 'ESP' (Columbia 1965) and 'Nefertiti' (Columbia 1967), amongst many others. Still active as a player, he has also worked extensively as a teacher and lecturer over the past two decades.

The Last Poets

Sometimes cited as the forebears of rap music, the group, consisting of Jalaluddin Mansur Nuriddin, Umar Bin Hassan, Abiodun Oyewole, Sulieman El-Hadi, as well as percussionist Nilaja Obabi, were characterised by a politicised and fiery vocal delivery that dealt with social issues of the day, whether accompanied by sparse percussion, or a full band. Jalaluddin was also responsible for the much sampled concept album 'Hustler's Convention' (United Artists 1973). Despite only releasing a handful of records, their influence endures. 'It's A Trip' from 'Delights Of The Garden' (Douglas 1977) continues to be a club favourite, and members of the group are still active today.

Elvin Jones

John Coltrane

There is little new that can be said about the genius of John Coltrane, a man who straddled the be-bop era, and the furthest reaches of the 'new music' or free jazz. He was the most successful bandleader of his time, and a supporter of fellow musical souls Eric Dolphy and Albert Ayler. Coltrane joined Miles Davis' group in 1955, and participated in the latter's recordings for Prestige, as well as the era defining 'Kind of Blue' (Columbia 1959).

He drew on these experiences when he became a bandleader, incorporating modes, as well as eastern motifs and scales into his arrangements and compositions. Coltrane honed his sound through albums like 'Giant Steps' (Atlantic 1960) 'My Favorite Things', (Atlantic 1961) and 'Africa Brass' (Impulse! 1961), as well as a string of live performances with different personnel. He eventually settled on Elvin Jones (drums), McCoy Tyner (piano) and Jimmy Garrison (bass) for his classic quartet from 1962 to1965.

In addition to his growing skills as a musician, Coltrane's spiritual ideas and philosophy developed in tandem with his creativity. Having struggled with drugs in the early part of his career, he attributed a spiritual experience to enabling him to beat his habit, the most profound expression of which was 'A Love Supreme' (Impulse! 1965) his most famous, and for many, greatest recording.

The dynamic of the band changed with the inclusion of saxophonist Pharoah Sanders, and drummer Rashied Ali. Both Tyner and Jones exited soon after, resulting in Coltrane's wife Alice stepping in to take care of keyboard duties. This final stage of his career saw Coltrane's vision expanding into ever-experimental territory, with a more spiritually charged sound on albums such as 'Interstellar Space' and 'Expression', both released in 1967, the year of Coltrane's death, as well as the posthumously released 'Cosmic Music'.

On these recordings there is a liquidity between the musicians, bubbling between the shards of interweaving notes and jagged percussion. Like many geniuses, Coltrane seemingly exited the planet too early and his final musical statements point to an affiliation with sound that reached far beyond a singular style or genre.

Roland Kirk

Leon Thomas

Famed for his full, baritone vocal, jazz singer Leon Thomas additionally utilised an African yodel style to add spiritual depth to many of his recordings like 'The Creator Has A Master Plan' or 'Hum Allah...', which he recorded with Pharoah Sanders. Born in 1937, he worked with Mary Lou Williams and Randy Weston before recording LPs with Sanders, and also in his own right, for Flying Dutchman. These included 'Spirits Known and Unknown' (1969), 'Blues and the Soulful Truth' (1972), and 'SNCC's Rap (1970) with H. Rap Brown, which appeared to consolidate political themes hinted at in his other work. He toured with Santana and even appeared on Louis Armstrong's last album. He worked again with Sanders in the 1980s, but his recording and live work became sporadic, and he passed away in 1999 from heart failure.

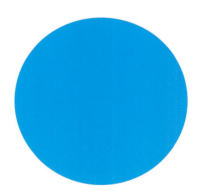

Muhal Richard Abrams

Born in Chicago in 1930, Muhal Richard Abrams, as a mostly self-taught composer and musician, cut his teeth as a sideman in the 1950s, working with people like Dexter Gordon and Ruth Brown. Although well-versed in hard bop and R&B, it was only when he assembled the Experimental Band in 1962 that he began to explore the freer musical realms that would make his name. The band ultimately morphed into the non-profit Association for the Advancement of Creative Musicians (AACM) in 1965, which Abrams was president of. From the 1970s onwards, he recorded and worked on solo projects, as well as composing within the classical and jazz field, for which he has received numerous plaudits.

Oliver Lake

Born in Arkansas in 1942, saxophonist and composer Oliver Lake has always pursued his own path as a musician. He founded the Black Artists Group (BAG) with Julius Hemphill and Charles 'Bobo' Shaw, a collective that spawned bands like The Human Arts Ensemble. In 1971, Lake recorded his self-financed debut 'Ntu: The Point From Which Creation Begins', which was eventually released in 1976 on Arista's Freedom label. After recording a number of solo albums, as well as touring Europe, Lake founded The World Saxophone Quartet with Hemphill, David Murray and Hamiet Bluiett, which he still performs with today, alongside numerous musical projects.

Gil Scott-Heron

Poet, singer, author and keyboard player, Scott-Heron was blessed with an earthy delivery and an acerbic skill in summarising the politics of the day. Born in Chicago in 1949, he initially recorded for Flying Dutchman, but it was on 'Winter In America' (Strata East 1974), an album which drew from R&B, blues and jazz so effortlessly, that he came to prominence when his single 'The Bottle' became a hit for the fledgling label. He subsequently signed to Arista, releasing a string of albums like 'The First Minute of a New Day' (1975) and 'Real Eyes' (1980). Through his spoken word recordings, like 'The Revolution Will Not Be Televised', he was also a major influence on hip hop culture. While a brilliant lyricist, it is sadly ironic that much of the dangers he warned against in his lyrics tragically caught him in later life. His final album 'I'm New Here' came out in 2011 one year before his death.

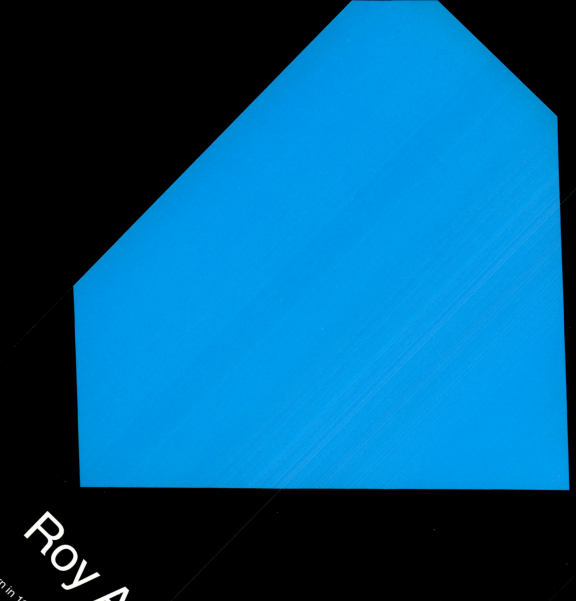

Roy Ayers

Born in 1940 in Los Angeles, vibraphonist and composer Roy Ayers grew up in a musical home, recording as a jazz artist for Atlantic. He utilise his sophisticated arrangement playing them to soul and funk music string of classic albums for He's Coming' (1971), 'Red, Black Everybody Loves The on to performing, he has

also produced artists for his own label Uno Melodic such as The Eighties Ladies and Sylvia Striplin, as well as spending time in Nigeria working with Fela Kuti. ('Music of Many Colors' Phonodisk/Celluloid 1980) – befitting of someone who's music often boasted a strong cultural and political edge. Still recording and playing today, his music has additionally borne a huge influence on hip-hop artists such as Pharrell and A Tribe Called Quest.

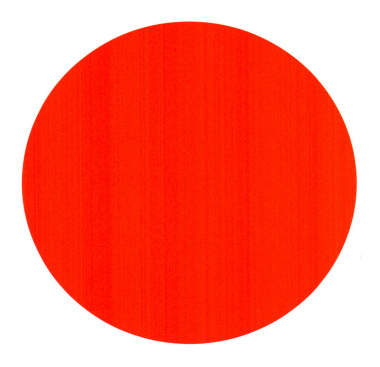

Wayne Shorter

Saxophonist and composer Wayne Shorter has packed a staggering career into one lifetime. Born in 1933, Shorter first gained attention with Art Blakey's Jazz Messengers, cutting several albums with him before joining Miles Davis' second great quintet, alongside Herbie Hancock and Tony Williams. He composed for Davis on albums like 'ESP' (Columbia 1965) and 'Nefertiti' (1967), as well as producing solo work for Blue Note, like 'JuJu' (1964). He played on Davis' groundbreaking 'In A Silent Way', but by the time Davis entered his full electric period in the early 1970s Shorter had started Weather Report with Joe Zawinul. Weather Report drew elements of jazz, rock and funk together, which became known as fusion, and featured the astounding Jaco Pastorious on bass. Shorter continued to work with the group, toured with Santana, and has latterly returned to working with a quartet.

Ornette and Denardo Coleman

Lonnie Liston Smith

Keyboardist Lonnie Liston Smith has a jazz pedigree that stretches back to his early work with Betty Carter, Rahsaan Roland Kirk and Pharoah Sanders. Born in 1940, he worked as a sideman for Leon Thomas and Miles Davis, before forming Lonnie Liston Smith and The Cosmic Echoes in the early 1970s, and recording key work for Bob Thiele's 'Flying Dutchman' label. Spacey funk with jazz overtones dominated his output during this period, with compositions such as 'Expansions' and 'Space Princess'. He contributed to Guru's 1993 'Jazzmatazz' project and is still active today.

AACM

Formed out of Muhal Richard Abrams' Experimental Group in 1965, the AACM's mandate of nurturing the creative vision of local artists as well as original, serious composition, has made it one of the most respected non-profit organisations of its kind today. Still offering free tuition to inner-city students in Chicago, as well as putting on performances and events, the organisation was founded by Phil Cohran, Steve McCall, Jodie Christian and Abrams, and includes Wadada Leo Smith, Henry Threadgill, George Lewis, Anthony Braxton and Art Ensemble of Chicago amongst its prestigious membership.

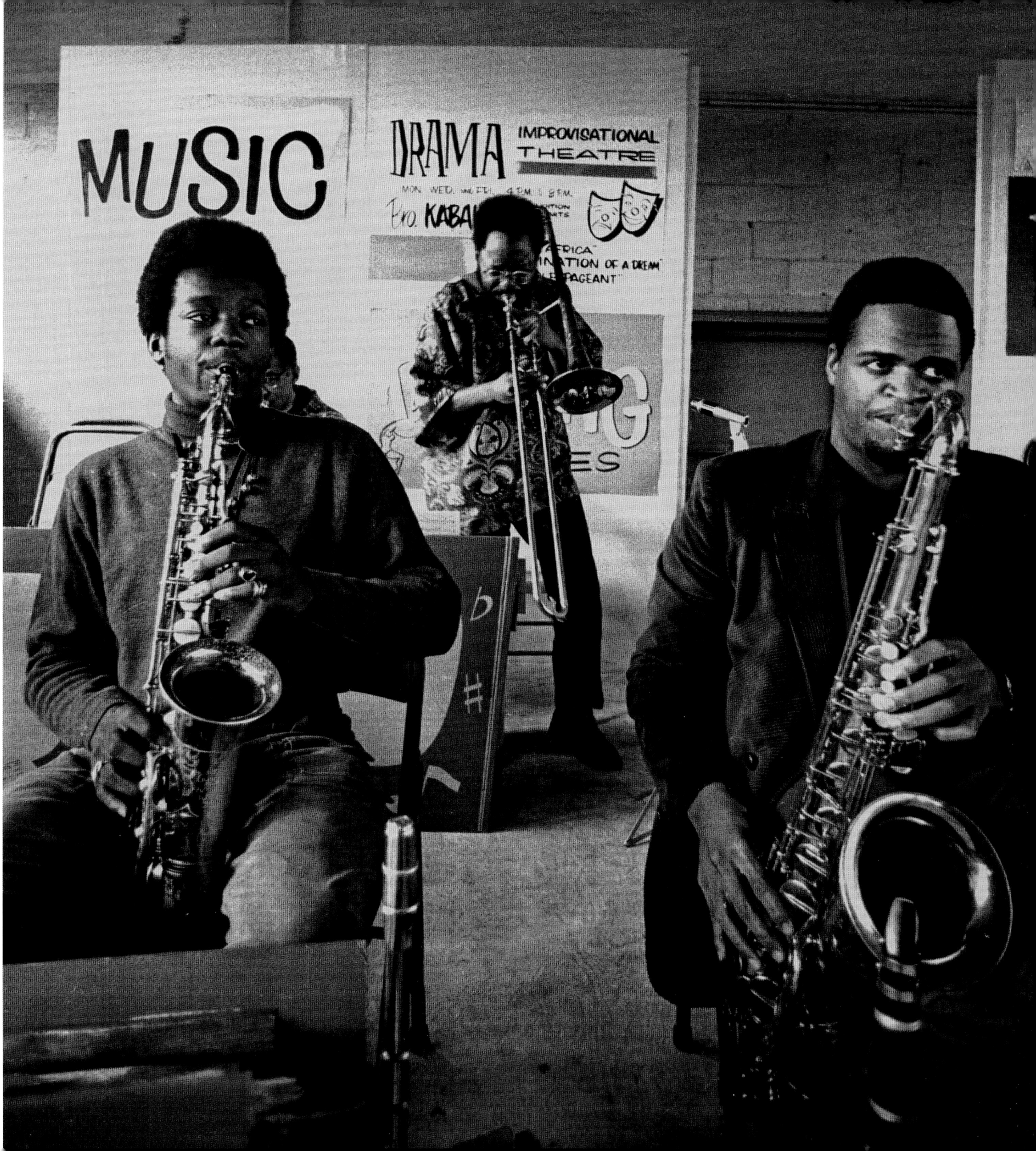
MUSIC
DRAMA
IMPROVISATIONAL
THEATRE

Donald Byrd

Trumpeter Donald Byrd enjoyed a varied and eclectic career evolving in each decade to reflect the musical trends of the time. Joining Art Blakey's Jazz Messengers in 1955 while still studying, he went on to record for Blue Note, releasing classics such as 'Fuego' (1960), 'A New Perspective' (1963) and 'Fancy Free' (1969). The focus of his music changed in the early 1970s when working with The Mizzell Brothers, who's soulful productions and arrangements bridged the gap between R&B and fusion. He also later made forays into disco with The 125th St NYC Band, producing the hit 'Love Has Come Around' (Elektra 1981) and rap, with Guru's 'Jazzmatazz' project. He taught and studied throughout his life, often involving his students in his recording projects. He died in 2013, aged 80.

Dee Dee Bridgewater

Jazz singer Dee Dee Bridgewater was born in Memphis in 1950 and sang from a young age. She first joined the Thad Jones-Mel Lewis Jazz Orchestra in the early 1970s and went on to work with Max Roach and Dexter Gordon amongst others. 1974 was a pivotal year as it saw the release of her classic 'Afro Blue' (Trio) as well as a leading role in the Broadway musical 'The Wiz'. She has recorded for Atlantic and Elektra and also appeared in other stage productions. She still performs regularly, touring the world over.

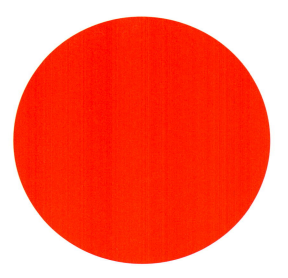

Miles Davis

Miles Davis was so forward thinking and prolific that it is difficult to summarise his musical career succinctly. Aside from his own talents at composing and playing trumpet, he had a knack for spotting talent, and consistently formed groups around him to support his musical vision.

Born in 1928, he replaced Dizzy Gillespie in Charlie Parker's quintet, eventually leading his own group on four albums for Prestige. He recorded his epoch defining 'Kind Of Blue' in 1959 for Columbia, which featured John Coltrane in the line up. With every track on this album there is perfectly poised and organic interplay between each band member, and the release proved a fine vehicle for Davis' growing skills as a player and composer. He followed this a year later, with the lyrical 'Sketches of Spain', the result of a burgeoning partnership with arranger Gil Evans who would become a regular collaborator.

His second great quintet featured Tony Williams (drums), Ron Carter (bass), Herbie Hancock (piano) and Wayne Shorter (saxophone), and he began to explore more open ended and modal structures with this group, as evidenced on 'Miles Smiles' (1967) and 'Filles De Kilimanjaro' (1968). In 1969 he released 'In A Silent Way', which consisted of two heavy modal tracks, further aided by producer Teo Macero's editing technique to shape the structure of the compositions, which set the tone for his next musical phase.

The seminal 'Bitches Brew' followed, with the album distilling Davis' interpretation of rock, funk and R&B, as well as a statement to those who might try and second-guess what jazz is. The 1970s heralded other key works like 'On The Corner', which showcased open-ended jams shot through with radical sentiment, and from this same period 'Get Up With It' (Columbia 1974). This creative drive was juxtaposed with health problems and substance abuse, which lead to erratic performances, and not much more was heard from Davis in the latter part of the 1970s.

His output lessened in the 1980s, but later albums like 'Decoy' (Warners 1984) and 'You're Under Arrest' (1985) continued to push the jazz envelope, the latter featuring two sweet interpretations of Cyndi Lauper's 'Time After Time' and Michael Jackson's 'Human Nature'. Davis would continue to write and perform up until his death in 1991.

Jimmy Smith

While not the first jazz musician to play the Hammond B3 organ, Jimmy Smith is most readily associated with this instrument and extended its possibilities and parameters as a player and composer. Born in Pennsylvania, he was signed by Blue Note's Alfred Lion the moment the latter saw him playing live, ushering in a string of albums for the label such as 'The Sermon!' (1958) and 'Back at the Chicken Shack' (1960). Smith's trademark was jazz-infused R&B with heavy improvisation, and he continued in this vein after he later signed to Verve Records. He worked alongside Kenny Burrell, Lou Donaldson and Tina Brooks, and played with Frank Sinatra and even Michael Jackson later in his career. Always an energetic performer, he continued to record and play live until his death in 2005.

Don Cherry

Born in 1936 in Oklahoma, Cherry first came to prominence working with Ornette Coleman, and he was one of the first wave of musicians to push the boundaries of improvisation and composition, which came to be termed 'Free Jazz'.

After leaving Coleman, Cherry's recordings and performances began to take in sounds and influences from different parts of Africa and Asia, and he spent extended periods in Europe. 'Eternal Rhythm' on MPS (1968), which incorporated gamelan and various wind instruments, proved a bridge to his future experiments on 'Organic Music Society' (Caprice 1972) and 'Brown Rice' (Horizon 1975). He would continue to work on and off with Coleman, as well as collaborate with artists like Lou Reed and Krzysztof Penderecki, up until his untimely passing in 1995.

McCoy Tyner

Born in Philadelphia in 1938, Tyner's solo career has spanned over four decades, though he initially came to prominence as part of John Coltrane's classic quartet. Having met Coltrane while still young, he eventually joined the group in 1960, playing on 'A Love Supreme' (Impulse! 1964), 'Crescent' (Impulse! 1964) and 'Live At The Village Vanguard' (Impulse! 1962) amongst others. Working with Coltrane introduced the pianist to new melodic concepts and ideas. 'Africa/Brass' (Impulse! 1961) displays his ample grasp of pentatonic scales and eastern modes, which would go on to distinguish his future playing.

After leaving the group in 1965, Tyner established himself as a gifted composer and bandleader, recording initially for Impulse!, then for Blue Note and Milestone, his developing style maturing on 'The Real McCoy' (Blue Note 1967), 'Time For Tyner' (Blue Note 1968), 'Extensions' (Blue Note 1970), the Grammy-nominated 'Sahara' (Milestone 1972) and the solo 'Echoes Of A Friend' (Milestone1972). On these and many others, his playing transcends genre and draws on classical technique, as well as musical ideas from across the globe.

In the early 1960s he also worked as a regular sideman with Donald Byrd, Bobby Hutcherson, Joe Henderson and Stanley Turrentine, as well as collaborating with George Benson and Cecil McBee in the latter part of his recording career. He still tours and plays regularly today.

Roland Kirk

Amira Baraka (LeRoi Jones)

Steve McCall (AACM)

Abbey Lincoln

Max Roach

Born in 1924 in North Carolina, Roach and his family moved to New York when he was four and he grew up during the Great Depression in Brooklyn. He learnt music from his aunt and sang in church, getting an early taste for drums playing for his local scout troupe. He was given his first kit aged 12, paying special attention to the technique of luminaries such as Chick Webb and Jo Jones, Count Basie's drummer.

His burgeoning career coincided with the inception of be-bop, and he played alongside Dizzy Gillespie in 1943 on early recordings with Coleman Hawkins' band. He graduated to Charlie Parker's legendary quintet with a youthful Miles Davis, who he also played for on 'Birth of Cool' in 1950. Eventually he formed his first quintet with Clifford Brown, and worked with Booker Little, Sonny Rollins and Donald Byrd, amongst others. Brown died in tragic circumstances, and as the 1960s

dawned there was a sharpening of Roach's music. Elements of his output started to become more politicised, beginning with the astonishing 'We Insist!', which featured his then wife Abbey Lincoln on vocals, as well as Nigerian percussionist Babatunde Olatunji. 'Percussion Bitter Sweet' followed in 1961, and Roach would continue to push boundaries with projects such as 'Lift Every Voice' on Atlantic (1971), which featured a full choir, and the harsh 'Force: Sweet Mao - Suid Africa '76' LP, a duet with saxophonist Archie Shepp.

His recordings with the M'Boom percussion group exemplify a musical openness that saw him experiment and collaborate in a broad variety of musical settings, in addition to enjoying a career in academia, until his passing in 2007.

Sam Jones

Born in 1924, bassist Jones moved to New York in 1955 and quickly became in demand as a sideman, working with Kenny Dorham, Lou Donaldson and Dizzy Gillespie. He is best known as part of Cannonball Adderley's quintet, appearing on 'African Waltz' (Riverside 1961) and 'Nippon Soul' (Riverside 1963). He also worked with Oscar Peterson for a period, and additionally recorded several albums as leader, such as 'Seven Minds' (East Wind 1974). He died in 1981.

Charles Tolliver

Charles Tolliver was born in Jacksonville, Florida. He first came to prominence in 1964, playing in Jackie McLean's group. In 1971, Tolliver and Stanley Cowell founded Strata-East Records.

As much as the Strata-East label was a conduit for releasing music outside of jazz's mainstream, it was also a radical statement in tune with the times. The music and product was mostly owned by the recording artists, and creativity over commercial gain was the priority. That said, the label had some success with Gil Scott-Heron's 'Winter In America' (1974), which spawned the hit single 'The Bottle', and they additionally released key material by Pharoah Sanders, Clifford Jordon, The Heath Brothers and JuJu (later Oneness of Juju).

After a long hiatus Tolliver re-emerged in the late 2000s, releasing two albums arranged for big band.

Anthony Braxton

Born in Chicago in 1945, saxophonist Braxton's music skirts between the avant-garde, classical and jazz scenes, though his music doesn't particularly belong to any of these. He was involved early on with the AACM, and has played with other members such as George Lewis and Wadada Leo Smith throughout his career, as well as luminaries like Sam Rivers and Dave Holland. He has been a teacher and professor of music for many years, and still records and performs today across different platforms.

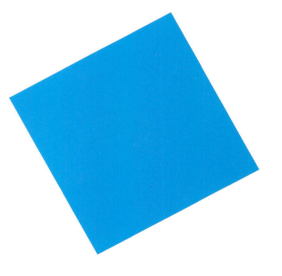

Eric Dolphy

Whilst multi-wind instrument player Eric Dolphy often gets dubbed 'avant-garde', in reality it was his advanced knowledge of different styles of composition that ensured his writing and playing stood out from early in his career, reaching a peak with 'Out To Lunch' (Blue Note 1964). Born in Los Angeles in 1928, he got his break working with Chico Hamilton, before moving to New York and joining Charles Mingus' Quartet in 1960. After touring Europe for a few months, he returned to New York and joined John Coltrane's group, recording with him on 'Africa/Brass' (Impulse! 1961). In his too short career he also worked with Booker Little, Ornette Coleman, Booker Ervin and Mal Waldron, and continued working with Mingus. He was on tour with him in Germany in 1964, when he died due to complications related to diabetes.

Tony Williams

Born in Chicago in 1945, drummer Tony Williams found fame early on when he joined the second of Miles Davis' classic quintets, aged 17 years old. He possessed a deftness of touch and subtlety way beyond his years and played on key albums with Davis, such as 'Miles Smiles' (Columbia 1966) and 'In A Silent Way' (Columbia 1969). During this time he also cut the excellent 'Life Time' (1964) and 'Spring' (1965) for Blue Note as leader, as well as playing on Eric Dolphy's 'Out To Lunch' (1964) and Herbie Hancock's 'Maiden Voyage' (1965). Post-Davis, Williams formed The Tony Williams Lifetime with guitarist John McLaughlin and Larry Young on organ, which moved further into fusion territory. He continued to play and record with the likes of Herbie Hancock and Jaco Pastorious, until an untimely death from a heart attack in 1997.

Stanley Cowell

Stanley Cowell was born in Ohio in 1945. Co-founder of Strata-East Records, he played with Roland Kirk while studying at the Oberlin Conservatory of Music. Cowell also played with trumpeter Charles Moore and others in the Detroit Artist's Workshop Jazz Ensemble in 1965-66, out of which later came Tribe Records and Kenny Cox's Strata label (not to be confused with Strata-East). He has also played alongside Marion Brown, Max Roach, Bobby Hutcherson, Clifford Jordan, Harold Land, Sonny Rollins and many others, as well as releasing numerous solo albums. He currently teaches at Rutger University.

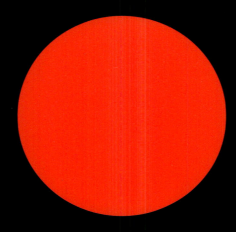

Sam Rivers

Born in 1923 in Oklahoma, Rivers was a serious composer and arranger who played several instruments including tenor saxophone, bass clarinet and flute. His playing was anchored in be-bop, but was easily capable of reaching out to jazz's outer margins. He recorded key albums for Blue Note such as 'Fuschia Swing Song' (1964) and 'Contours' (1965), and went on to be a leading light in the 1970s 'loft jazz' scene in New York. He recorded and performed until his passing in 2011, seemingly never tiring of pushing the creative envelope.

Art Blakey

One of the few drummers to truly explore the furthest percussive reaches of his instrument, Blakey's thunderous hard-bop style felt as rooted in the West African coast as it did the clubs of New York. Born in 1919 in Pittsburgh, he started work as a pianist, but soon switched to drums, playing with Chick Webb and Mary Lou Williams.

A trip to Africa in 1948 proved pivotal in his musical and philosophical development, after which he converted to Islam for a time. Whether consciously or otherwise, Blakey re-interpreted African poly-rhythms for the jazz idiom, be it on early recordings such as 'Art Blakey with the Original Jazz Messengers' (Columbia 1956) or the more explicit 'Holiday For Skins' (Blue Note 1958) and 'The African Beat' (Blue Note 1962), and was capable of a staggering dynamic range. As both a sideman and band leader, Blakey worked with the greats, including Miles Davis, Thelonious Monk and Horace Silver, and his evolving group The Jazz Messengers proved a training ground for a broad school of musicians past and present, right up unti his passing in 1990.

Horace Silver

As a pianist and composer, Horace Silver has carved out a rich and creative lineage in jazz. From his earliest work as a leader alongside Art Blakey with The Jazz Messengers to his ground-breaking 'United States of Mind' trilogy on Blue Note, Silver has always drawn deeply from his musical heritage. Born in 1928, his talent caught the ears of Blue Note executives, and he worked with the label until 1980. He drew on his Cape Verdean background for 'Song For My Father' and referenced the blues and gospel in many of his compositions such as 'Serenade To A Soul Sister' (1968). There are subtle political undertones to his work with Andy Bey on the 'United States...' trilogy and 'Silver n' Percussion' (1978) explored cultural themes in his music. He is a true pioneer, innovator and one of the jazz's elder statesman.

Duke Pearson

Producer, pianist and composer Pearson was born in Atlanta in 1932. A child prodigy, he left the army in the mid-1950s, moving to New York where he came to the attention of Donald Byrd. He played on Byrd's 'New Perspective' (Blue Note 1963) as well as contributing his composition, 'Cristo Redentor'. He then started working as A&R for the label while also continuing to record solo works, releasing 'Wahoo' (1964) and 'The Phantom (1968), amongst other notable works. In addition to working with Blue Note, he also recorded 'Prairie Dog' for Atlantic in 1966, and 'Dedication!' for Prestige in 1970. He continued to work and teach until 1980, when he died from multiple sclerosis.

Lee Morgan

The gifted trumpeter Lee Morgan was at home on his own material such as the R&B tinged 'The Sidewinder', as he was working as sideman with Grachan Moncur III, Wayne Shorter and many others. Born in 1938, he recorded prolifically for Blue Note as a leader, and also recorded significant work as part of Art Blakey's Jazz Messengers. 'The Sidewinder' was his most commercially successful track, but not content to merely repeat this formula he began to explore deeper, modal territory on albums like 'Search for the New Land' (1964) and 'The Procrastinator' (1967). He had begun to adopt a more political stance at the turn of the 1970s, when tragedy struck and he was shot dead by his common-law wife during an altercation in a nightclub. He was just 33 years old.

Joe Henderson

Born in Ohio in 1937, saxophonist Henderson moved to New York after serving in the army, beginning a fruitful relationship with Blue Note both as a sideman, where he worked with Herbie Hancock and Andrew Hill, as well as leading on solo albums like 'Inner Urge' (1964) and 'Mode For Joe' (1966). From 1967, he produced equally crucial work for Milestone, resulting in the classic 'The Elements', (1973) which featured Alice Coltrane, and 'Black Narcissus' (1976). He would continue to work and perform, until his death in 2001.

Black Artists Group

Inspired by the AACM and the Black Arts Movement, the Black Artists Group was formed in 1968 in St. Louis. Between 1968 and 1973 the group, whose focus was to inspire local collaboration and co-operation between experimental artists, counted Oliver Lake, Julius Hemphill, Charles 'Bobo' Shaw, actor Ajule Rutlinand and Hamiet Bluiett among its membership. It was unique as it attempted to draw the worlds of theatre, dance, the visual arts and film into its orbit. In the early 1970s the group, following the lead of The Art Ensemble of Chicago, moved to Paris where they recorded their sole album 'In Paris, Aries 1973' (Bag 1973). They split up shortly afterwards with much of its membership then pursuing successful solo careers.

David Newman

Tenor saxophonist David 'Fathead' Newman, was born in Texas in 1933. After building up a reputation playing locally, he joined Ray Charles' band in 1954, where he stayed for ten years. After this he embarked on a successful solo career with Atlantic records where he also recorded many significant dates as a sideman with artists such as Aretha Franklin, Dr. John, Eddie Harris and BB King. Later, he continued to record as leader for High Note and was playing and performing until his death in 2009.

Cecil Taylor

Pianist Cecil Taylor, long cited as a pioneer of free jazz, drew from his classical training, applying melodic and rhythmic complexities to his playing. Born in 1929, his dense and percussive approach proved challenging from the outset to a world only just recently adjusted to be-bop. Aside from some early work as a sideman, he has mostly led his own groups from the 1950s onwards. His collaborators have included Jimmy Lyons, Archie Shepp and Sunny Murray. From early albums on Candid, Contemporary and Blue Note, such as 'The World of Cecil Taylor' (1960) and 'Units Structures' (1966) up to the present, Taylor's playing and interaction with fellow musicians have consistently challenged the boundaries of jazz. Ever the pioneer, he recently sought funding to turn his house into a living museum.

Marion Brown

Born in Atlanta in 1931, saxophonist Marion Brown moved to New York at the turn of the 1960s, a crucial time for the 'new thing', and soon gravitated toward its leading lights such as Ornette Coleman, Sun Ra, Pharaoh Sanders and John Coltrane, playing on 'Ascension' (Impulse! 1965). The following year he released 'Three For Shepp' (Impulse!) and continued to record throughout the rest of the decade and into the 1970s. After a sojourn in Paris, he involved himself increasingly in academia, as well as working with Harold Budd and Steve Lacy. He died in 2010.

Jimmy Smith

John Coltrane

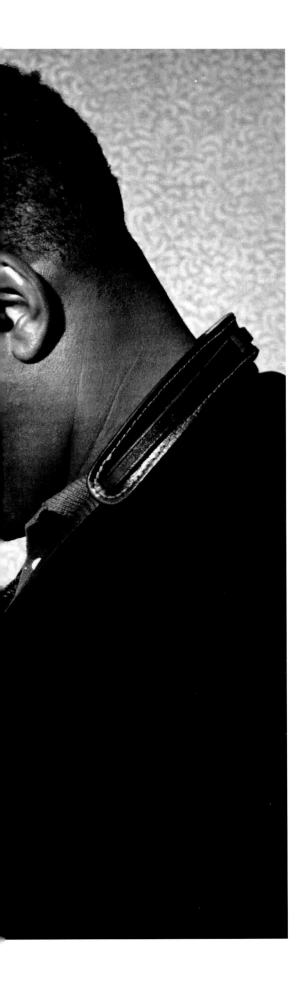

Cecil Taylor

Andrew Hill

Despite a string of albums as bandleader for Blue Note and others, the prolific pianist and composer does not generally receive the credit he deserves. Born in Chicago in 1931 to Haitian parents, his musical career began as a soprano singer, as well as attending talent shows where he would also play the accordion and tap dance. Charlie Parker was a friend of his father, and gave Hill his first gig. After a series of dates as a sideman in both Los Angeles and New York, Hill began to establish himself in his own right in the early 1960s. Blue Note's Alfred Lyon saw him as his last great protégé, and over a three year period recorded Hill on a startling string of albums including 'Point of Departure' (1964), 'Judgement' (1964) and 'Compulsion!!!!!' (1965).

In 1969 he recorded the beautiful and lyrical 'Passing Ships', a project shelved until it was released in 2003 to great acclaim. The latter exemplified Hill's forward thinking approach as a player and composer, gleaning him plaudits toward the end of his career. He continued to work up until his death in 2007.

Thelonius Monk

One of the giants of modern jazz, Thelonious Sphere Monk was born in 1917. Initially often misunderstood, he developed his unique, percussive piano style playing at Minton's Playhouse in New York, which brought him into contact with the emerging talents of Charlie Parker and Dizzy Gillespie. Initially mentored by Mary Lou Williams, her influence can be heard on early compositions like 'Epistrophy' and 'Brilliant Corners', now rightly hailed as groundbreaking, but which at the time seemed beyond jazz's regular vocabulary. Some musicians would sometimes criticise Monk due to not being able to actually play the complex pieces that he'd written. After early work with Blue Note and Prestige, Monk signed to Riverside in the mid-1950s where his fortunes improved and his talent further recognised. He led a residency at the Five Spot featuring John Coltrane, who was later replaced by Charles Rouse, and he went on to record several live albums for Columbia. Less active from the mid-1970s onwards, the reclusive behaviour that followed a long tour was attributed to mental illness. He passed away after a stroke in 1982.

Ramsey Lewis

Born in Chicago in 1935, composer and pianist Ramsey Lewis is perhaps best known for his crossover hits such as 'The In Crowd' and 'Wade In The Water' recorded on the Argo/Cadet labels in the 1960s . A hugely successful artist, Lewis moved into fusion in the 1970s with a string of classic albums such as 'Sun Goddess' (Columbia 1974) and Salongo (Columbia 1976) produced by Charles Stepney and Earth, Wind & Fire's Maurice White, both figures who also began their careers at Chess in the 1960s. Lewis still performs today and also has a successful career in television and radio.

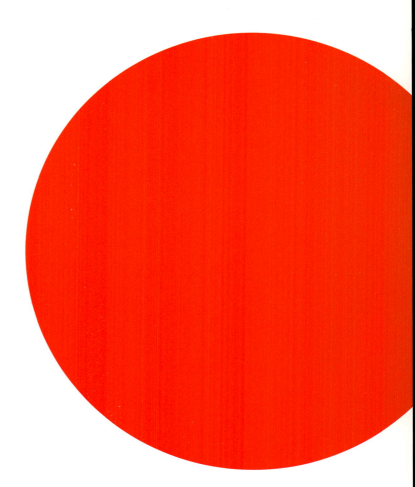

Leroy Jenkins

Born in 1932, composer and violinist Jenkins was part of the AACM and was known for expanding the sonic boundaries of his instrument, be it exploring classical techniques in his playing through to more organic sounds and drones. He spent time in Paris, but returned to America in 1970, forming The Revolutionary Ensemble with bassist Sirone and percussionist Jeremy Copper. In addition, Jenkins worked with Alice Coltrane, Archie Shepp and Anthony Braxton during this period, and cut LPs for India Navigation and Black Saint. Jenkins also worked as a teacher as well as performing for theatre productions and as musician-in-residence at different universities. He died in 2007.

Tribe

Tribe were one of the most important independent collectives and record labels on the American underground jazz scene. Formed in Detroit in the 1970s, members included Phil Ranelin, Wendell Harrison, Harold McKinney and Marcus Belgrave (pictured). Their musical approach was broad, taking inspiration from figures like Coltrane and Archie Shepp, while also infusing their productions with funk and soul extrapolations, though always with an avant-garde slant. Though Tribe's philosophy was avowedly uncommercial, several musicians associated with the label did session work for Motown. They also produced a community magazine, focussing on social and political issues of the day. Key releases include 'Message From The Tribe' (1973), Wendell Harrison's 'An Evening With The Devil' (1973) and Marcus Belgrave's 'Gemini II' (1974). Many members are still active today, with some collaborating with electronic musician Carl Craig on the project 'Tribe Rebirth' in 2009.

Lloyd McNeil

Washington DC born McNeill is an independent artist, as proficient on the flute as he is as a painter. From 1968-73 he ran his own Asha label and self-released many of his recordings and compositions. In the 1960s he studied in Europe, where he befriended Picasso, and has worked with Ron Carter and Cecil McBee as well as Brazilian musicians like Dom Salvador and Nana Vasconcelos. There is a warm lyricism to McNeill's playing and compositions, and he has taught, exhibited his drawings and paintings, and published his own poetry. Two of his early albums 'Asha' and 'Washington Suite', long out of print, were recently reissued by Soul Jazz.

Larry Young

Larry Young, one of the freshest innovators on the Hammond B3 organ, was born in Newark in 1940. With a background in R&B, Young began recording for Blue Note in 1964, which also marked a change in his style and approach, bringing a more intricate and subtle technique to an instrument most readily associated with the gutsy blues of Jimmy Smith. Beginning with 'Into Somethin'' in 1964, Young released a handful of recordings for the label, concluding with the masterful 'Mother Ship' in 1969. In the next decade he associated with the emerging fusion sound, working with John McLaughlin, Tony Williams and Miles Davis, and eventually releasing 'Lawrence of Newark' (Perception 1973) and the definitive, spaced out R&B of 'Fuel' (1975 Arista). He died in 1978.

Stanley Turrentine

Born in 1943, saxophonist Stanley Turrentine didn't stray far from the R&B tinged jazz that he cut his teeth on in the 1950s with Earl Bostic and Lowell Fulson. After a stint with Max Roach, he married organist Shirley Scott, performing with her, as well as with the legendary Jimmy Smith. He released several albums on Blue Note in a similar vein, like 'Hustlin'' (1964) and 'Joyride' (1965), and found further success in the 1970s on the CTI label with 'Sugar' (1970) and 'Don't Mess With Mister T' (1973), the former being a key release for both artist and label. Further albums followed on Fantasy, and Turrentine continued to record and perform up until his death in 2000.

Hubert Laws

Hubert Laws was born in Texas in 1939. He grew up in a musical family with many of his siblings becoming professional musicians, including saxophonist Ronnie and vocalists Eloise, Debra and Johnnie Laws. He played with the early Jazz Crusaders (later The Crusaders) in Texas before moving to New York to study at the Juilliard School of Music. Whilst studying he began playing in Mongo Santamaria's group in the evenings. In the 1960s Laws played with classical orchestras, signed to Atlantic as a solo jazz artist and session player (and later CTI), where he uniquely fused jazz, latin, soul and classical styles. He continues to perform today, and in 2010 received a lifetime achievement award from the National Endowment for the Arts.

Charles Lloyd

Born in Memphis in 1938, saxophonist Lloyd's early experience was steeped in the musical culture of this most significant of cities. Playing initially with local groups, he moved to California in 1956, working with Eric Dolphy, Ornette Coleman and Bobby Hutcherson, and eventually as a regular with Chico Hamilton and Cannonball Adderley. His fame as a player and band leader took off after his group's appearance at the Monterey Jazz Festival, and his subsequent 'Forest Flower' LP (Atlantic 1966). He shared stages with some of the biggest rock acts of the day, such as Jimi Hendrix and Cream, which also bore influence on his compositions. After taking a break in the 1970s, Lloyd returned to music, recording for ECM, an association that endures to the present day.

Freddie Hubbard

One of the most outstanding trumpet players of his generation, Hubbard made his solo debut for Blue Note at only 22 with 'Open Sesame' (1960). In addition, he had significant work as a sideman for Art Blakey, Wayne Shorter and Herbie Hancock, as well as several albums as leader for Atlantic and Blue Note. He had further success, with Creed Taylor's CTI label, with albums like 'Red Clay' (1970) and 'First Light' (1972), which earned him a Grammy. He was honored with the Jazz Masters award by The National Endowment for the Arts in 2006, its highest accolade for jazz, two years before his passing.

Sonny Rollins

Rollins is rightly cited as one of the most influential tenor saxophonists in jazz. Born in 1930 in New York, he first played with Miles Davis, JJ Johnson and Bud Powell, and recorded his breakthrough compositions 'Oleo' and 'Doxy' in this initial period. He then worked with Max Roach and Clifford Brown, before eventually leading his own group. He recorded for Prestige and Blue Note in the 1950s, releasing 'Tenor Madness' (Prestige 1956), 'Way Out West' (Contemporary 1957) and 'Newk's Time' (Blue Note 1958). Over the next decade he would work for long periods then drop out altogether (such as when he visited India to study yoga), but always returned with renewed vigour as heard on albums such as 'The Bridge' (RCA Victor 1962). After another sabbatical, he began a long and fruitful association with Milestone Records releasing numerous titles such as 'The Cutting Edge' (1974) and 'Don't Stop The Carnival (1978). In the 1980s he even worked with The Rolling Stones. He continues to play and record regularly, turning out inspiring performances up to the present day.

Stanley Clarke

Born in Philadelphia in 1951, bassist Clarke moved to New York in
1971 and immediately began working with the likes of Joe
Henderson, Horace Silver and Pharoah Sanders. His break came
through working with Chick Corea, as part of the pioneering fusion
band Return to Forever. In addition to solo work, such as 'School
Days' (Nemperor 1976), he collaborated with Billy Cobham amongst
others. Clarke continues to record and perform today, with a latter
focus on music for film and television.

Steve Reid

Drummer Steve Reid was an amazing musician, as at home in the avant garde scene as he was working with James Brown or cutting sessions at Motown. Born in 1944 in the South Bronx, he played drums from the age of 16, working in the house band at the Apollo under Quincy Jones, as well as travelling around Africa after graduation. On these travels he encountered and played with Guy Warren, Randy Weston and Fela Kuti. He spent time in jail on his return for avoiding the draft for Vietnam, but upon his release formed The Legendary Master Brotherhood and his own Mustevic label,

releasing his own work as well as recordings by Charles Tyler, and David Weterman. During this time he also worked with Sun Ra, Sam Rivers and Gary Bartz. He was recording and playing live into the 1990s, when he enjoyed a well-deserved second-wind in his career, hooking up with Kieran Hebden aka Fourtet. Over a handful of studio LPs, and inspiring live performances, the two traded an almost telepathic rhythmic fluidity underlining Reid's ability to adapt to any musical setting. This partnership was sadly cut short when Reid passed away in 2010.

Horace Tapscott

Despite his talent as a pianist and composer, Horace Tapscott rarely gets the recognition he deserves. Born in Houston in 1934, his family relocated to Los Angeles, where he would remain for most of his life. At the turn of the 1960s, an association with the avant-garde as well as community activism, contributed to his forming the Underground Musicians' Association (UGMA) and the Pan Afrikan Peoples Arkestra, which focused on preserving African-American music and culture. He performed live with the Arkestra, and elsewhere as band leader, releasing several titles on the Nimbus label, as well as 'The Giant Is Awakened' on Flying Dutchman (1969). There was greater awareness of his talent toward the end of his life, and he toured with the Arkestra in the 1990s, before his death in 1999.

George Benson

While best known for crossover songs in the late 1970s such as 'Give Me The Night', Benson was a prolific jazz guitarist, before moving into the pop R&B mainstream. Born in Pittsburgh in 1943, he recorded solo albums for Prestige and Columbia, as well as working with keyboardists Brother Jack McDuff, Lonnie Smith and Larry Young. He played on Miles Davis' 'Miles in the Sky' (Columbia 1968) and shortly afterwards signed to CTI, releasing early fusion albums such as 'White Rabbit' (1971). In 1976 he took part in two recordings for Paul Winley credited to the Harlem Underground Band, which spawned the much-sampled 'Smokin' Cheeba Cheeba'. In the same year he played on Stevie Wonder's 'Songs In The Key of Life', and upon signing to Warner Brothers moved further into the mainstream, releasing 'Breezin'' (1976) and 'Give Me The Night' (1980), which was produced by Quincy Jones. His stellar career continues to the present day, with contributions to Masters of Work 'Nuyorican Soul' project in 1996, which introduced his talents to a new generation of listeners.

Bobby Hutcherson

A unique and inventive vibes player, Hutcherson has probably done more to show the instrument's creative possibilities than anyone else in jazz. Born in Los Angeles in 1941, he ended up staying in New York after the group he was with were invited to play at Birdland. As a sideman and leader, he had one of the most enduring relationships with Blue Note out of his contemporaries. Be it adding angular, melodic touches to Eric Dolphy's 'Out To Lunch' (1964) or on his own stand out LPs like 'Components' (1965), 'Now!' (1969) or 'Montara' (1974), Hutcherson's playing remained accessible, though always left-of-centre to keep his audience guessing, an approach he has continued to apply to his live and recording work up until the present day.

Cannonball Adderley

Born in 1928 in Florida, saxophonist and composer Adderley moved to New York in the 1950s where he was soon spotted by Miles Davis. Joining Davis' sextet, he played on the seminal 'Kind Of Blue' in 1959. Soon after this he began leading his own group, which included Yusef Lateef, Sam Jones and Joe Zawinul. He then signed to Capitol where he began a long-lasting working relationship with David Axelrod, who produced numerous titles for him such as 'Live At The Club' (1967), which contained the crossover hit 'Mercy, Mercy, Mercy', 'Accent On Africa' (1968) and 'Country Preacher' (1969). Adderley continued to record, perform and experiment during this period. He died in 1975.

Ahmad Jamal

Born in 1930, pianist and composer Jamal is considered one of the more influential musicians of his generation due to his technique and evocation of space and depth in his playing. A child prodigy, he toured with George Hudsons's Orchestra prior to a move to Chicago, which also coincided with his conversion to Islam. His band The Three Strings, which evolved into the Ahmad Jamal Trio, came to the attention of producer John Hammond who signed them to Okeh. 1958 saw the release of the hugely popular '...at the Pershing: But Not For Me' (Argo), which contained Jamal's composition 'Poinciana'. Jamal toured North Africa, then moved to New York after his group disbanded. He continued playing and releasing albums like 'Extensions' (Argo 1965), 'The Awakening' (Impulse! 1970) and 'Outertimeinnerspace' (Impulse! 1972), which saw Jamal expand his style, as well as utilise the Fender Rhodes alongside his regular piano. He has continued to perform and record regularly, enjoying a renewed interest in his work from the 1990s to the present day.

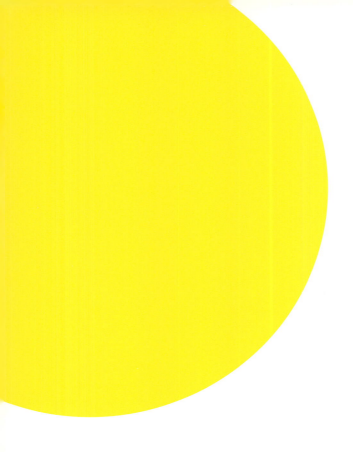

Pheeroan akLaff

Born in 1955 in Detroit, drummer and percussionist Pheeroan akLaff (Paul Madoxx) has retained a long standing association with the independent jazz scene. In Detroit he was a contemporary of Tribe members Wendell Harrison and Marcus Belgrave, and in New York took lessons from Coltrane quintet member Rashied Ali, and Herbie Hancock sideman, Billy Hart. As well as his own solo recordings he worked with luminaries of the avant-garde like Oliver Lake, Travis Biggs, Henry Threadgill and Waddada Leo Smith. He still plays and records today, and in 2006 set up the non-profit, Brooklyn-based, Seed Artists Inc.

Joseph Jarman

Primarily known as an AACM founder as well as member of Art Ensemble of Chicago, saxophonist Jarman, like contemporaries Anthony Braxton and Henry Threadgill, has always stuck to his own musical path, with a strong intellectual and philosophical undercurrent to his work. In addition to his AECO discography he has recorded several albums as leader such as 'Song For' (Delmark 1966) and 'The Magic Triangle' (Black Saint 1979). He still plays today while additionally practicing as a Buddhist priest.

Chico Hamilton

Up until his death aged 92 in 2013, Chico Hamilton's career encompassed an astoundingly broad musical spectrum. From backing Billie Holiday or Lena Horne, to working with Charles Mingus, Sammy Davis Jr., Lionel Hampton and Duke Ellington, not to mention his own groups, soundtrack work and commercials. He was one of the pioneers of the West Coast jazz scene, cutting albums for Pacific Jazz, as well as Impulse! and Black Saint. In addition to being a prolific band leader, his groups served as a training ground for several younger talents like Eric Dolphy, Dexter Gordon and Charles Lloyd, amongst many others.

Frank Lowe

Born in Memphis in 1943, saxophonist Frank Lowe had a long career as an improviser and stalwart of the 'new thing', working with Sun Ra, Alice Coltrane and Don Cherry. He was most prolific in the 1970s and early 1980s, releasing several LPs as leader, sometimes independently, as with his classic album 'Duo Exchange' (Survival Records 1973) with Coltrane collaborator Rashied Ali. After a break, he continued to work regularly, including on the Thurston Moore produced 'Out Of Nowhere' (Ecstatic Peace 1993). He died in 2003.

George Duke

Born in California in 1946, Duke played in a number of different groups whilst studying, eventually forming the house band with Al Jarreau at the Half Note in San Francisco. Whilst best known for his fusion work, and hits like 'Brazilian Love Affair', he has worked across the musical spectrum both as sideman, leader, composer and producer, be it part of Frank Zappa's Mother of Invention, Cannonball Adderley's band or his groundbreaking trio with violinist Jean-Luc Ponty. He continued working, playing and writing up until his passing in 2013.

Lonnie Smith

Born in 1942, and with a background in R&B and gospel, Hammond organ player and composer Smith moved to New York in 1966 where he first worked with guitarist George Benson, recording his first album as leader, 'Finger Lickin' Good', for Columbia a year later. Smith then began a fruitful collaboration with Lou Donaldson and subsequently signed to Blue Note, where he developed his signature jazz-tinged R&B, on albums like 'Move Your Hand' (1969) and 'Drives' (1970). He went on to record for Kudu and Groove Merchant, where his sound evolved further. He still performs live and records today.

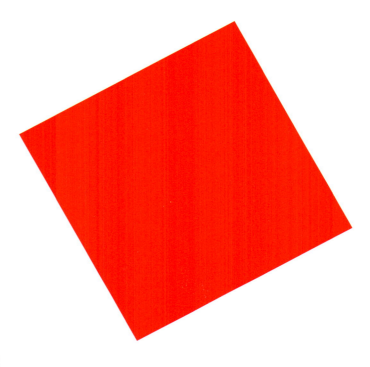

Charlie Mingus

A serious composer regardless of genre, jazz is nonetheless the arena that bassist Charlie Mingus worked within, often straying over its boundaries, with his compositions and playing drawing deeply on his own musical experiences. Born in 1922 in Arizona, he was a musical prodigy, touring with Louis Armstrong in the 1940s before working with Charlie Parker in the 1950s. This was followed by one of his most prolific periods, recording key works like 'Pithencanthropus Erectus' (Atlantic 1956), 'Mingus Ah Um' (Columbia 1959) and the masterful 'The Black Saint and The Sinner Lady (Impulse! 1963). Mingus had a fiery reputation, often resulting in on-stage altercations and he frequently burnt professional bridges. Despite this, he collaborated with numerous musicians like Max Roach, Booker Ervin, Rahsaan Roland Kirk, Clifford Jordan and Eric Dolphy, and he continued to record and perform, pushing his own musical parameters and those of his personnel. Less active in the final phase of his life, he was eventually diagnosed with motor neurone disease and was working on an album with Joni Mitchell when he passed away in 1979.

Bobbi Humphrey

Bobbi Humphrey is one of the most successful female jazz instrumentalists, and began recording for Blue Note as the label's focus shifted to releasing more fusion and R&B-based material at the start of the 1970s. Born in 1950, and learning her trademark flute in school, she recorded a series of solo albums for the label such as 'Blacks and Blues' (1973) and 'Satin Doll' (1974), as well as albums for Epic. She has also worked with Duke Ellington and Stevie Wonder and still performs today.

Gary Bartz

Born in Baltimore in 1940, Bartz was playing saxophone from his late teens, and by the early 1960s had already landed side work with Max Roach and Art Blakey. His recordings as band leader, underpinned by a strong cultural and philosophical ethos, established him as a unique artist in his own right, such as the two volumes of 'Harlem Bush Music' (Milestone 1970 & 1971) and the seminal 'I've Known Rivers' (Prestige 1973) with regular collaborator Andy Bey. He also participated in lesser know avant-garde sessions like Mtume's 'Alkebu-Lan' LP on Strata East as well as having a crossover hit with 'Music Is My Sanctuary' (Capitol 1977). In 2005 he was awarded a Grammy for his playing on McCoy Tyner's 'Iluminations' and is still recording and playing today.

Phil Upchurch

An all-round guitarist and bass player in the R&B and jazz tradition of his hometown of Chicago, Phil Upchurch has worked with a huge range of musicians including Curtis Mayfield, B.B. King and Dizzy Gillespie, as well being part of The Soulful Strings and Rotary Connection, both groups who recorded for Chess Records in the late 1960s. Born in 1941, he is equally at home as either sideman or leader on his own projects, illustrated by his 1961 hit 'You Can't Sit Down', his quartet work with Tennyson Stephens and solo albums such as 'The Way I Feel' and 'Upchurch' both made for Chess in 1969. His work with Rotary Connection on tracks such as 'I Am the Black Gold of the Sun', has proved enduring, and he still performs today.

Bobby Timmons

Within his brief career, pianist Bobby Timmons consolidated and built on his gospel and church background, infusing this sensibility into his style that was dubbed 'soul jazz' at the time. Born in 1935 in Philadelphia, he was a contemporary of the Heath Brothers and had early success writing 'Moanin" for Art Blakey while he was part of the Jazz Messengers, as well as 'This Here' and 'Dat Dere' for Cannonball Adderley. In the early 1960s he led his own trio with Tootie Heath on drums and Ron Carter on bass, cutting LPs for Riverside and Prestige. Sadly this success was combined with an increased consumption of alcohol and narcotics, and he died of cirrhosis of the liver in 1974.

Nathan Davis

Whilst saxophonist and composer Davis' discography is quite minimal for someone born in 1937, each release has a purpose, and arose from context and conscious choices made by one of jazz's most fiercely independent artists. Preferring Europe to the US, after leaving the army Davis based himself in Paris, working with Kenny Clarke, Eric Dolphy and Art Blakey, as well as recording as leader on albums like 'Happy Girl' (Saba 1965) and 'Rules of Freedom' (Polydor 1967). He returned to America in 1969 to take up a position at the University of Pittsburgh, and has since divided his time between academia (he has a Ph.D in Ethnomusicology) and teaching. Thankfully, he still found time for occasionally recording, including seminal albums like 'If' (Tomorrow International 1976) and heading up the Paris Reunion Band with musicians like Joe Henderson and Johnny Griffin, which brought his work full circle.